True Acting Tips

Larry Silverberg

True Acting Tips

A Path to Aliveness, Freedom, Passion, and Vitality

Larry Silverberg

An Imprint of Hal Leonard Corporation

Published in 2012 by Limelight Editions
An Imprint of Hal Leonard Corporation
7777 West Bluemound Road
Milwaukee, WI 53213

Trade Book Division Editorial Offices
33 Plymouth St., Montclair, NJ 07042

Printed in the United States of America
Book design by Mayapriya Long, Bookwrights

All photos are from Shutterstock
Library of Congress Cataloging-in-Publication Data is available upon request

ISBN 978-1-4584-1376-5
www.limelighteditions.com

For Jill

Contents

Preface

On November 8, 2010, I began a column on my website called "True Acting Tips." I was urged to do the tips by a friend and colleague, Art at Artotems Co., who has been working with me on my Internet activities for many years. I was reluctant at first to do tips, because I have never been a fan of easy fixes when it comes to the craft of acting. After giving it some thought, however, I decided to use this forum as a place to investigate, with readers, ways of working that are demanding, provocative, and deeply human. As the tips evolved, the column became a place where I have been able to share the technical aspects of acting technique as well as the more philosophical and spiritual backbone that lives inside acting, life, and the way we live our lives.

What a wonderful surprise when, very quickly, the tips gained a global following. I have been inspired to keep writing the tips by countless emails of appreciation I have received from people in many parts of the world who have found them useful and who read them religiously. Of course, I was overjoyed when the kind folks at Limelight Editions told me that they were enthusiastic about the tips and that they would publish them as my newest book on acting.

In Part One you will find 203 tips, exploring key themes that I examine from many different angles. I have assignments for you to explore, as well as many ideas for you to reflect on. Between each tip, you will find an inspirational quote, offered here to instigate further thought about the relationship between our humanity and the art of acting. (Thanks to Artotems Co. for their contribution of some of the inspirational quotes.)

In Part Two, True Actor Resources, I present three people whom I thought you would enjoy knowing and who have very good information to support you and your acting activities.

If you have any questions about the material presented in the tips, suggestions for new tips, or anything you would like to share with me in response to these tips, please contact me via my website: www.trueactinginstitute.com.

Part One

True Acting Tips

~1~

A primary True Acting value: Embrace everything, deny nothing.

> "The right word may be effective, but no word was ever as effective as a rightly timed pause."
>
> —Mark Twain

~2~

Someone may come up to you and say, "Wow, how do you remember all those lines?" But for the True Actor, memorizing the words is the very least of the challenges.

*"Today you are You, that is truer than true.
There is no one alive who is Youer than You."*

—Dr. Seuss

~3~

True Acting is much more about learning how to ask your-self great questions than about having great answers.

"I feel the capacity to care is the thing which gives life its deepest significance."

—Pablo Casals

~4~

Do not confuse yelling with actually doing something on-stage. I have seen so many plays where the actors scream at each other throughout the whole performance. Believe me, there are an infinite variety of ways to accomplish your "action," and the least important of these is the volume of your voice!

Why, then, are so many actors yelling? It is because, in many acting classes, the expression of anger is actually promoted and praised. There are teachers who turn anger into the holy grail of acting. And students who feel good getting into that state of rage fall into the trap. What a sad mistake for everyone involved.

Remember, all human expression is good, and when you are fully present, available, and free, you will always respond appropriately to the needs of the moment. And you may indeed get angry or sad or joyful. The vital point is that you must always be fully responding to the needs of the moment, wherever they lead.

The problem is when acting students are manipulated into becoming angry for anger's 'own sake and at the expense of everything else. This is what we then see on the stage, actors screaming at each other at the expense of everything else—including their acting partners and acting itself.

"The emotions aren't always immediately subject to reason, but they are always immediately subject to action."

—William James

~5~

All human behavior is purposeful. The same must be true on the stage.

"Only in spontaneity can we be who we truly are."
—John McLaughlin

True Acting demands a total devotion. At the expense of everything else? No! By welcoming everything else.

"Adversity has the effect of eliciting talents, which in prosperous circumstances would have lain dormant."

—Horace

~7~

In human beings, words are the last thing to occur. They arise out of a deep-seated desire. Actors must have the very same authentic need to say the words, or their life onstage is without true purpose.

> "Nothing ever happened in the past; it happened in the Now. Nothing will ever happen in the future; it will happen in the Now."
>
> —Eckhart Tolle

~8~

All human beings are connected by an "invisible thread." Because most people have their attention only on themselves, the invisible thread is severed. The actor's attention must be directed outward so that the invisible thread remains intact.

"I have been impressed with the urgency of doing. Knowing is not enough; we must apply. Being willing is not enough; we must do."

—Leonardo da Vinci

~9~

Attention on oneself, acting is not possible. Attention directed to the other, acting is possible.

*"A black cat crossing your path signifies
that the animal is going somewhere."*

—Groucho Marx

~10~

True Acting is an art of "Authentic Relationship." This is rare in life, so of course, it is rare on the stage.

"Curiosity is one of the permanent and certain characteristics of a vigorous mind."

—Samuel Johnson

~11~

One of the greatest traps for the actor is when you look for emotional results. It creates a paralyzing "watching your-self," and your instrument can't function. So what must you do? Look at Tip 12 for insight.

"It is our attitude at the beginning of a difficult undertaking which, more than anything else, will determine its successful outcome."

—William James

~12~

Important to notice. In life, no one sits around trying to be emotional. Only badly trained actors do. Simply, our emotions are a response to our attempts to do things in life that are vitally important to us. This, of course, is the basis of the realm of the emotions and how they relate to True Acting. When you make an authentic attempt to accomplish something that is actually meaningful to you, it has an impact on you that is out of your control. And that's what we want! This way, you are not trying to do the emotion, it's doing you.

"To be nobody but yourself in a world doing its best to make you everybody else means to fight the hardest battle any human can ever fight and never stop fighting."

—e. e. cummings

~13~

A very important thing to adhere to when on the set is to not talk about how you work—just do the work.

"I know who I am and who I may be, if I choose."

—Miguel de Cervantes

~14~

At the first read-through of the play, many directors will encourage the cast to "act" the parts from day one and to give fully realized performances immediately. Of course, this is impossible. And most actors will comply, "indicating," pretending and faking their way through the read-through.

Why do these directors do this? Because they have no understanding of the actor's process and are terrified that if the cast is not brilliant from the first rehearsal, the production will be a disaster. Here's the tip. At the first read-through, do not cave in to the pressure all around you to "perform"; stay simple and take the time you need in rehearsals to do the real work that needs to be done.

"Logic will get you from A to B. Imagination will take you everywhere."

—Albert Einstein

~15~

In musical theater, the song must be an attempt to accomplish something vital and specific. And the need to accomplish it must be so important that there is nothing left to do but to sing it out! This dynamic is missing in many musical-theater productions, but when it is present, it takes your breath away.

*"The most essential factor is persistence—
the determination never to allow your
energy or enthusiasm to be dampened by the
discouragement that must inevitably come."*

—James Whitcomb

~16~

From Playing Ball on Running Water, by David K. Reynolds, the three fundamental principles: "Accept your feelings, know your purpose, and do what needs doing."

*"I want you to be everything that's you,
deep at the center of your being."*

—Confucius

~17~

It's not the words you say, it's the music you play.

"We are cups, constantly and quietly being
filled. The trick is, knowing how to tip ourselves
over and let the beautiful stuff out."

—Ray Bradbury

~18~

Acting is an "act of creation" and, like all acts of creation, it is ultimately a mystery. The True Actor has worked relentlessly to become strong, willing and able to allow that which is miraculous to occur.

"The greatest gift is a portion of thyself."
—Ralph Waldo Emerson

~19~

In life, it is easy to fall in to that sleep state called "living an assumption." But True Actors know that one must never assume anything, because in every moment, anything is possible.

"Kindness in words creates confidence.
Kindness in thinking creates profoundness.
Kindness in giving creates love."

—Lao Tzu

~20~

In life, most people expend a great amount of energy trying to control things that they have no control over. True Actors have learned that onstage, just like in life, there is only one thing that they actually have the ability to control. What is it? It is what they do. And they willingly, and joyfully, give up control over everything else.

"Do you have patience to wait till your mud settles and the water is clear? Can you remain unmoving till the right action arises by itself?"

—Lao Tzu

~21~

Here is a valuable quote: "The greatest gift we can give to another is the quality of our attention." This is a key to healthy and fulfilling relationships in our lives, so of course it is a basic and vital tenet of True Acting.

"It is ever the invisible that is the object of our profoundest worship. With the lover it is not the seen but the unseen that he muses upon."

—Christian Nestell Bovee

~22~

You are driving on the highway. Suddenly, the driver of the car in front of you hits his breaks. Instantly, without any thought, you check over your right shoulder, see that the lane to the right is clear, swerve into the right lane, hit the gas pedal, speed past the crazy driver, look over your left shoulder and see that the crazy driver is behind you, steer back into your original lane, and then resume your normal speed. This is called "adjusting to what is actually happening as it is happening." In life we do this all the time. Yet it is quite rare on the stage. Why? Let's continue with the highway analogy . . .

When you drive on the highway, do you drive the car based on how the traffic was yesterday? No—that would be silly. You drive the car based on what the traffic condition is right now. Unfortunately, many actors drive their car based on how the traffic was yesterday--meaning they try to reproduce what worked at the first read-through, or they use moves that they rehearsed at home in front of the mirror. This is why a lot of theater is so lifeless and why, if you look around at the audience, you will see many people who have literally gone to sleep or are busy texting their sisters! (And these people sleeping and texting during the play will be the first to jump to their feet to give a standing ovation at the curtain call.)

True Acting is an art of presence, meaning the life of your acting is in working with the truth of the moment right now and what is actually happening right now. So, clearly, "adjusting to what is actually happening as it is happening" is a major ingredient in our craft.

"The artist who aims at perfection in
everything achieves it in nothing."
—Eugène Delacroix

~23~

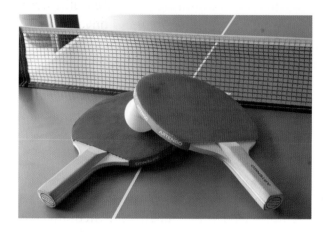

Due to the urgent nature of this acting value, I am continuing with the word "adjusting." When you watch amazing championship Ping-Pong players hitting the ball back and forth at a hundred miles an hour, do you imagine that it is possible for them to think about where to place the paddle? Of course not! If they did, the ball would go right by them. There's no time to think. So, to be effective, Ping-Pong players have refined their skills to the point where they are in continual, moment-by-moment adjustment to the opponent and to the continually changing path of the ball, and always without any thought whatsoever.

As actors, we don't have a table and ball. What we have are the infinite variety of subtle new things that are happening in our partners' behavior every night onstage, and these, too, are coming at us at a hundred miles an hour. True Actors, just like Ping-Pong players, after rigorous years of work on their craft, have claimed the ability to adjust instantly, spontaneously, and organically to everything the partner is dishing up to them, in every moment.

"Between stimulus and response there is a space. In that space is our power to choose our response. In our response lies our growth and our freedom."

—Viktor E. Frankl

~24~

Sanford Meisner called it "the reality of doing." When you do something, you must actually do it rather than try to make it look like you are doing it. This key to True Acting springs from the fact that the only way to reach an audience "where they live" is through the actor's authentic experience in the moment.

"There are no failures—just experiences
and your reactions to them."

—Tom Krause

~25~

Just like life itself, "desire" is the fundamental building block of the craft of True Acting.

"And while I stood there I saw more than I can tell and I understood more than I saw; for I was seeing in a sacred manner the shapes of all things in the spirit, and the shape of all shapes as they must live together like one being."

—Black Elk

~26~

Most actors learn to listen only with their ears. This is not true connection at all. The True Actor learns to listen with the "ear of his heart."

"Stories are the secret reservoir of values:
change the stories individuals and nations
live by and tell themselves, and you change
the individuals and nations."

—Ben Okri

~27~

Before every performance, Rudolf Nureyev would work himself out to the point of exhaustion. He said he did this so that he would have "nothing left to hang on to and then he would soar!" The True Actor has cultivated the very same way of working.

"We always weaken everything we exaggerate."

—Frederic-Cesar La Harpe

~28~

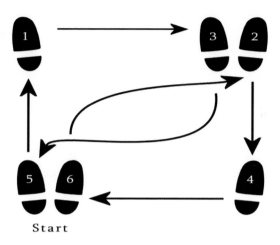

Start

Learning the craft of acting is a three-steps-forward, one-step-backward, four-steps-forward, two-steps-backward kind of process. It is useful to know that it is always "the two steps backwards" that makes the next leap forward possible.

"Imagination will often carry us to worlds that never were. But without it we go nowhere."

—Carl Sagan

~29~

Strive to get yourself out of the way, to become an empty vessel, so that the character is free to speak through you.

"No tears in the writer, no tears in the reader. No surprise in the writer, no surprise in the reader."

—Robert Frost

True Acting is an art in which you cannot stop to corroborate what you have just created. When you do, you are no longer acting. You are doing something unrelated to acting.

"Think left and think right and think low and think high. Oh, the thinks you can think up if only you try!"

—Dr. Seuss

~31~

Here's a tip . . . Read *On Directing* by Harold Clurman. For actors and directors, it is the clearest and most useful investigation of script analysis ever written.

"Things won are done, joy's soul lies in the doing."

—William Shakespeare

~32~

You cannot make an audience believe you; you can only invite them to share your experience. Remember this vital truth: an audience always knows when they are being lied to.

"Beyond a doubt, truth bears the same relation to falsehood as light to darkness."

—Leonardo da Vinci

~33~

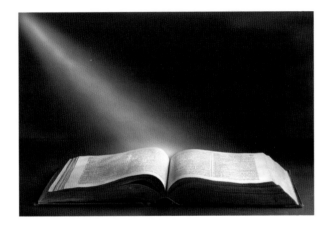

The script is your bible; it is your source of inspiration to take action. Every choice you make must be justified by what you find in the text; if it is not, you have no right to that choice.

"With me poetry has not been a purpose, but a passion."

—Edgar Allan Poe

~34~

When many actors think about playing a "character," they think about adding a limp or a bad case of stuttering. The truth is, limping and stuttering do not make a character. "Character," simply defined, is a specific point of view, how the person "sees" the world. Now, if you tell me that having a limp or a bad stutter affects a person's point of view toward the world around them, I say to you, "Now you are on to something!" Let's explore some more on this topic in the next tip.

"It's not just a question of conquering a summit previously unknown, but of tracing, step by step, a new pathway to it."

—Gustav Mahler

~35~

What really is a "character" role? Think of a character as a person who is wearing a pair of sunglasses with purple lenses. Everything they see, obviously, will be purple. With a non-character role, the person can take in information, evaluate it, and choose how to respond appropriately. "Characters" do not have the ability to evaluate and choose. Everything that they encounter is filtered by the specific set of lenses through which they see the world. We call this a "specific point of view," and that is the most useful definition of the acting element called "character." Your job, should you choose to accept it, is to authentically inhabit the character's point of view so that you begin to see the world through those very same colored lenses. No easy task, but what fun!

"Sincerity is moral truth."

—George Henry Lewes

~36~

The actor knows, yet he must not know. So how do you "not know" when you "already know"? There is only one way. If you are fully immersed in the present moment, the next moment takes you by surprise. See? You really don't know.

"To be conscious means not simply to be, but to be reported, known, to have awareness of one's being added to that being."

—William James

~37~

The performance is not supposed to be merely a repeat of the night before or of what you did in rehearsals. And your understanding of the character is not supposed to be over and done with by opening night. Each night, your relationship with the character must deepen. The play, too, is supposed to be a living, breathing organism that evolves and grows over time. How? As a result of you and the other actors working well.

Of course, what we are talking about is a very rare event. So do your part! Strive to keep the play alive even though you may be working with people who have gone onto automatic pilot. You will stand out like a lighthouse on a very dark sea.

"When you swim you don't grab hold of the water, because if you do you will sink and drown. Instead you relax, and float."

—Alan Watts

~38~

A pause in talking onstage is not a technical thing. Unfortunately, many directors do not understand this. (This is why productions of Pinter's plays are so often unbearable and without life.) A pause in speech onstage, like in life, occurs because something has happened that makes talking impossible. So even though the characters are not talking at the moment, they are still involved in something that they are doing—in other words, something they are trying to accomplish. You, the actor, must be involved in the same thing.

And if the director tells you to take a long pause, which he might do without any good reason, you must figure out how to justify that long pause; you must know what you are doing—specifically—that makes it impossible to speak.

Marcel Marceau said, "Isn't it true that the most meaningful moments in our lives leave us speechless?"

—Great insight for actors.

"Education is not the filling of a pail,
but the lighting of a fire."

—William Butler Yeats

~39~

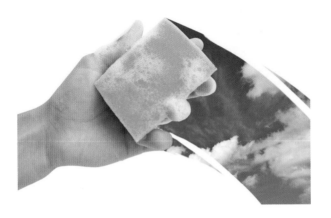

When you are acting in a play, every night before the per-formance, make sure there's no garbage in the theater, no candy wrappers by the seats, no programs on the floor, no sticky stuff on the armrests. Care that much.

"Knowing your own darkness is the best method for dealing with the darknesses of other people."

—Carl Jung

Here's a typical conversation:

Carol: Bob, I am trying to tell you that this is really important to me, and you are not even listening.

Bob: I am listening.

Carol: No you're not, you have not heard a single thing I've said.

Bob: I hear you, I hear you.

Carol: Oh, this is just a waste of time. I really give up—I give up!

The truth is that Bob was not really listening, he was thinking about taking his car in to the mechanic because it is making a rattling sound whenever he presses down on the gas pedal. Now, Carol, didn't know that Bob was thinking about his car problems, but she did know in her gut that he was not really giving her his full attention.

And also true, and very sad, is that Bob is not even conscious of the fact that he is not really listening to Carol—that he has no true connection with her—because this has become the thick fog he lives in every moment of his life. When Bob is at work, he thinks about playing basketball. When he plays basketball, he thinks about having meatloaf for dinner. When he eats his meatloaf, he thinks about looking for a good deal on bookshelves at Walmart. When he shops for bookshelves, he thinks about the time he asked his boss for a raise and was refused. And on, and on, and on . . .

So Bob is never really involved with anything he is doing in his life. He is actually not living a moment of his life at all. Bob has gone to sleep, you see? He is, in fact, sleepwalking through his life.

True Acting is a process of waking up, of reconnecting with the world around you by giving your full attention to the people you are with and to what you are doing in every moment. It's not enough to do it on the stage; it is a life practice. We are after something big here, really big.

"Negativity can only feed on negativity."
—Elisabeth Kübler-Ross

~41~

The concept of "talent" should be of no concern to you. We really know nothing about it—it is a gift and is out of your control. The only thing that is your concern and is in your control is working very hard, because when you do, you create the opportunity to fulfill the gifts you have been given.

"I believe the greatest gift I can conceive of having from anyone is to be seen by them, heard by them, to be understood and touched by them. The greatest gift I can give is to see, hear, understand and to touch another person. When this is done I feel contact has been made."

—Virginia Satir

~42~

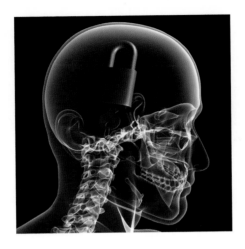

Every actor learns how to "play an action." Very few deal with "why" they are playing that action. I do not mean why the character is doing it—that's easy, as it's in the text. What I mean is, why are you doing it? In life, we do things for a reason. So does the character. It is only actors who very often have no real reason for doing the things they are doing onstage. When this happens, there is no life and there is no true character.

"There are many spokes on the wheel of life.
First, we're here to explore new possibilities."

—Ray Charles

~43~

If you can't fall in love with the character, you can't play the part.

"Art is not a handicraft, it is the transmission of feeling the artist has experienced."

—Leo Tolstoy

~44~

When you start to work on the role, rather than highlighting your lines of dialogue with a highlighter, rewrite the entire script by hand. Not on a computer—actually rewrite the entire script with pencil and paper. And take out all of the punctuation and the stage directions. They are unnecessary and just give the mind more ways to get in the way of the creative process.

Something wonderful happens when you do all this initial preparation of the script by hand. You are laying the foundation for making the text your own. Yes, it is just the very beginning of the work, but an important one, and down the road there will be a payoff for the extra work you put in at the beginning.

"By failing to prepare, you are preparing to fail."
—Benjamin Franklin

~45~

Acting is not a "Me, myself, and I" form of art. The True Actor knows that it is the other members of the team who will carry him or her to the ultimate heights of creation, where the greatest joys reside.

"The only real failure in life is not to be true to the best one knows."

—Buddha

~46~

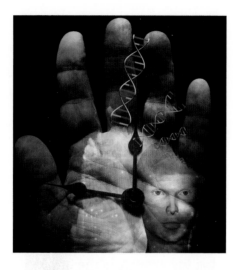

When you really know the difference you can make as an actor, in reminding people at a very deep level that they are, in fact, human beings, then you will start to understand the urgent need to bring True Life to the stage.

"The heart surrenders everything to the moment.
The mind judges and holds back."

—Ram Dass

~47~

For the True Actor, the answer to the question "What time is it?" is always, "Right now!" (from Suzanne Shepherd)

"Without a sense of urgency, desire loses its value."

—Jim Rohn

~48~

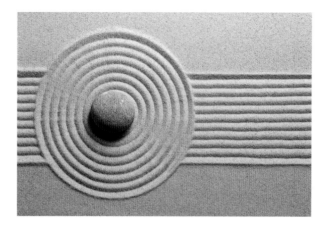

The mark of all great artists is that they make it look simple, like they are not really doing anything, as if it is as easy as breathing. When I watch Isaac Stern play the violin, I think I can play that well, too! True Actors continually strive to achieve simplicity in their work, so there is nothing extraneous, nothing extra.

"Where there is shouting, there is no true knowledge."
—Leonardo da Vinci

~49~

Take a hard and honest look at the things you are trying to accomplish in your life and the attempts you make every day to get closer to the fulfillment of these desires. Dig beneath all general thinking and get absolutely specific with yourself. When you do, you are also learning how to look into the heart of the characters you play.

"A work of art is the unique result of a unique temperament."

—Oscar Wilde

~50~

When you work on a role, your first reading of the script is very important. Read in a relaxed and quiet space. Notice how the mind immediately starts to figure out exactly how you will perform this part—notice this and let it go. Simply allow the circumstances and the words of the script to begin to work on you, to speak to the place in you that knows more than the mind. Make no conclusions about anything, no decisions about what might work and what won't work. It's too early for any of that.

"With the past, I have nothing to do;
nor with the future. I live now."

—Ralph Waldo Emerson

~ 51 ~

Here's a great group warmup for the whole cast of the play you are in. Every day, get to the theater early and do a line rehearsal. Do the line rehearsal in this manner . . . Bring a little ball with you, stand in a circle, and throw the ball to each other with energy! As you throw the ball rapidly around the circle, say the words of the play "by rote" and as fast as you can. "By rote" means without any acting. Just get those words out fast. Go through the lines of the whole play without any pauses. If anyone gets stuck, screws up a line, or pauses, the group must start again at the beginning of the play.

When you finish the line rehearsal, go to your dressing room and sink into that place called "the point of view of the character" and prepare yourself for another great roller-coaster ride out onstage tonight. When you have a cast of actors who are willing to go the extra mile, this is a wonderful way to work with each other before every show.

"To be persuasive we must be believable; to be believable we must be credible; to be credible we must be truthful."

—Edward R. Murrow

~52~

You must build your whole world on the stage you will be acting on. Here's an insightful story for you. One of my great teachers, Suzanne, was directing a production of an Athol Fugard play. The lead actress, April, wanted a fragrant flower called hedychiums placed into a pewter keepsake box that she kept on the dressing table. This dressing table was part of the set, and April sat at it many times during the play. So Suzanne asked the stage manager to get some hedychiums and put them into the silver box. The next day, Suzanne checked the silver box and the flowers were not there. Again, she asked the stage manager to arrange for the flowers and place them in the box for the next day of rehearsals. The next day, once again, the flowers were not in the box. This time, Suzanne was upset and asked the stage manager why she still had not arranged for the flowers and placed them in the box. The stage manager replied, "She doesn't need them—she never opens the box during the play!" Suzanne told her, "It is not for the audience. It is for the actress."

You must build your own, very specific world on that stage you will be living on—not for the audience but so that you have a personal relationship with this place. This will result in surprising, authentic, and human behavior, which will contribute to a reality onstage that will draw the audience into your experience and help them forget that they are sitting in a theater watching a performance.

"No man is an Island, entire of itself; every man is a piece of the Continent, a part of the main; if a clod be washed away by the sea, Europe is the less, as well as if a promontory were, as well as if a manor of thy friends or of thine own were; any man's death diminishes me, because I am involved in Mankind; And therefore never send to know for whom the bell tolls; It tolls for thee."

—John Donne

~53~

In your performances, do not look to repeat what you did last night. You can't step into the same river twice.

"Man is fond of counting his troubles, but he does not count his joys. If he counted them up as he ought to, he would see that every lot has enough happiness provided for it."

—Fyodor Dostoevsky

~54~

When you play a role, you must take the character out into life. Wear your costume and go to the deli and order a sandwich; go to a coffee shop and talk to the waitress. Soon it won't feel like a costume anymore. I have seen many performances where it is obvious that the actor has no relationship to the clothes he is wearing. Where would your character go to buy a shirt? Go there. Go there and talk with people, and ask for help finding some clothes. Find other creative way to explore your role out in the world. Do all of these things as you sink deeper and deeper into your character's point of view. Is this "method"? No, it's imaginative, and it's fun—and it is crucial that you adopt the character's point of view not only in the circumstances of the play, but toward the whole world around you.

"As an artist, I feel that we must try many things—but above all we must dare to fail."

—John Cassavetes

~ 55 ~

Documentary film alert: For Once in My Life.

If you are an actor, an artist in any medium, a teacher at any grade level, a human being, you must see this film. For Once in My Life is a documentary about a unique band of singers and musicians, and their journey to show the world the greatness—and killer soundtrack—within each of them. The twenty-eight band members have a wide range of mental and physical disabilities, as well as musical abilities that extend into ranges of pure genius. In a cinema vérité style, the film explores their struggles and triumphs, and the healing power of music, as the band members' unique talents are nurtured to challenge the world's perceptions.

The film is also about a great teacher, music director and creative director Javier Peña, who shows very clearly that effective teaching is not the expounding of facts and data, but rather it comes from a deep availability to every student and truly caring for their growth and well-being.

Unfortunately, many of the most important and inspiring documentary films produced are not seen by a wide audience. I urge you to buy the DVD and see it, show it to friends, and, if you are a parent, ask your child's teacher to show it in class or in an assembly to the whole school.

"Appreciation can make a day—even change a life. Your willingness to put it into words is all that is necessary."

—Margaret Cousins

~56~

Many actors complain, "I can't work with this person—they are not giving me anything." Of course, this is never true. The other person may not be giving you what you want, but they are always giving you something. Just like when Ed goes on a blind date and comes home and says to his roommate, "That girl has no personality!" That's not true, right? The girl may not have had the personality he would have preferred, but she certainly had some sort of personality. Same in acting. When it comes to human behavior, there is never nothing; there is always something.

"One can never consent to creep when
one feels an impulse to soar."

—Helen Keller

~57~

If you are onstage and you have a bowl of cereal to eat, eat it! But many actors sit there holding a spoonful of cereal, waving it in the air while they talk to the other actor and never eating the cereal. I have seen this countless times, the actor never eating the food because they are too busy saying the words and they do not want the food to get in their way of having a "really good moment." Hey, if you are supposed to be eating, put your attention on what you are doing and eat the food.

"A lot of my best parts I've been the second choice for, so you never get too egotistical about anything."

—Michael Caine

~58~

When you learn your lines, never speak them out loud until you are in rehearsals with the other actors. That's right, I said not to say the words out loud at all when you are by yourself. Resist the pull to make any decisions about which words need emphasis, what the tempo should be, when to take dramatic pauses, et cetera . . . Just leave it all alone! Leave it all alone or you will cripple your performance, guaranteed.

"It is a miserable state of mind to have few things to desire and many things to fear."

—Francis Bacon

~59~

This whole thing we are investigating together, this thing called True Acting, must become effortless. Effort causes strain, and strain makes it more difficult or impossible for your instrument to function. I am not saying it isn't the most grueling and difficult work. I am saying that at a certain point you stop doing "it" and "it" does you. When you get yourself out of the way completely, you will be taken by storm in ways that you could never have imagined, and that's what we want! Then, and only then, do you enter the creative arena. Is this rare? Yes. Is it worth striving for? Oh, yes.

"All human actions have one or more of these seven causes: chance, nature, compulsions, habit, reason, passion, desire."

—Aristotle

The word "tactic" is widely used in the acting classroom, and it is a word that leads actors (of any age) to the most unfortunate bad habits and artificial ways of working. Here's what many actors do with this idea of tactics. They go home, they practice their tactic, and then they come to rehearsal and "do their tactic" on their partner exactly as it was planned out at home. This continues into the performances, always "doing their tactic" on their partners exactly as it was done in rehearsals, which was exactly as it was carefully planned out at home. Do you have a sense yet of what is missing in this equation? It is the other person!

This is a vast and huge problem in the training of actors, and it's happening in acting classrooms on every continent on this planet. Actors are being trained to choose a tactic, practice it at home, and then "do it" on their partners, but the partner might as well not even be there. This is an intellectual approach to working with "objectives" and the "playing of objectives," and it is totally unrelated to human life as we know it. It is also one of the keys to why many productions make us want to stand up from our seats and scream, "What the hell am I doing here? I can't stand this and I have to get out of here!" This is so important, let's continue with it in the next tip.

"When it is obvious that the goals cannot be reached, don't adjust the goals, adjust the action steps."

—Confucius

~61~

A deep examination and exploration of the script leads to understanding what the character is trying to accomplish in every moment of the play. Some people call these the "actions" or "objectives"; I like to call them "doings." So this is part one, knowing what you are doing. Then there is the flip side of the very same coin, which is "how" you go about doing it. This is what many acting teachers and actors like to call "tactics," and this is probably the worst possible word for a very simple and human acting component. It brings up images of generals sitting around the war room, strategically planning out an attack on the enemy. And that's exactly how most actors approach the "playing of an action."

Discovering "how you do" what you have to do cannot be realized by yourself at home. You may ask, "Then how do I figure out how to do the doing?" Once again, this question suggests that you are trying to handle a nonintellectual challenge in an intellectual way. To lead you to the solution, let's look at an example from life.

You come home and as you enter the kitchen, your lover is standing by the sink, the water running, and she is crying in deep sobs and wiping her eyes with a towel. You rush over to her and throw your arms around her, but she pushes you away with great force and screams out, "Don't! Don't!" Now, do you imagine that you will immediately rush right back over to her and throw your arms around her in the very same way? No, of course you won't, you're a human being and you would "adjust" to the information you just received from her response. You might keep your distance and whisper gently, "What happened, honey?" or maybe you would remain silent for a while. The only person who would rush right back over and throw his arms around her in the very same way would be the actor who had carefully and strategically rehearsed his "tactic" at home by himself!

Is it all a little clearer now? In the next tip, let's get even more specific.

"We have two ears and one tongue so that
we would listen more and talk less."

—Diogenes

From the kitchen story you read the previous tip, you might have surmised the simple answer to the question we have been exploring: "How do I figure out how to do the doing?" Here it is in the clearest way possible.

Yes, you must always know specifically what you are doing, but the "how" to do it is given to you by the other person. Of course, this means you must be the kind of actor who can actually receive what the other actor is giving to you. You must also be the kind of actor who can then authentically respond to that behavior, moment by moment by moment. Develop these True Acting skills and you gain the ability to enter the unknown, which is, of course, the only place true creation is possible.

"The shortest answer is doing the thing."

—Ernest Hemingway

~63~

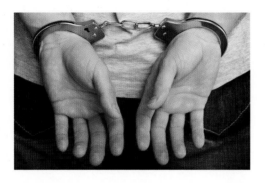

Many actors onstage complain and worry, "What should I be doing with my hands?" Of course, this is a problem only for actors who have their attention on themselves. When your attention is directed outward, the hands will do what they do in the most natural and relaxed way and will be of no concern whatsoever. As will the rest of your behavior. You see, there is a great relaxation of the mind as it shifts gently aside so that you can do your work. The ability to have your attention on the world around you 100 percent of the time corrects many acting problems in one grand sweep. Now, that's exciting!

"Your vision will become clear only when you can look into your own heart. Who looks outside, dreams; who looks inside, awakes."

—Carl Jung

~64~

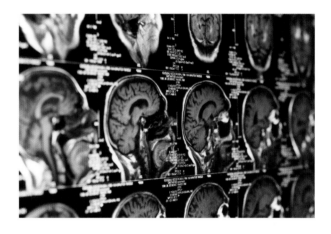

Anyone can read the words of a play and tell you the basic storyline. Just about everyone can look at their own x-ray and tell you, "Oh, yes, those are the bones, that is my spine," et cetera. But a chiropractor, after years of grueling study, has developed the ability to look at the very same x-ray and tell you a lot about your life! True Actors have been trained in the skill of "x-raying" the script; they have become deeply sensitized to the life that is waiting "inside" the words.

"I hold that the perfection of form and beauty is contained in the sum of all men."

—Albrecht Dürer

~ 65 ~

I now reintroduce an urgent matter. There is what I call an "invisible thread" that connects all people. It always exists; we just forget. It usually takes extreme circumstances to remind people of this connection. Onstage, when you are working well, this invisible thread will remain intact. If at any moment you become unavailable to your partners or the world around you, you cut the thread—and it must not be severed! When it is severed, you are no longer engaged in True Acting; you become involved in something totally unrelated to True Acting and certainly of no interest to your partners or to the audience.

> "Success is blocked by concentrating on it and planning for it . . . Success is shy—it won't come out while you're watching."
> —Tennessee Williams

~66~

As a student of what I call True Acting, you must be prepared to be unreasonable with yourself. "But," you say, "the only time we can rehearse is after I get off work at eleven p.m. and I am really tired." Then be really tired and get yourself to your rehearsal. "But," you say, "that means that I have to bring all of my props for the scene to work with me, and they're heavy, and my scene partner lives all the way across town and there is too much snow on the streets." Then schlep your props to work and then schlep them all the way across town, through the snow, and get yourself to your rehearsal. "But," you say, "almost nobody in class is putting in the kind of effort you are suggesting!" Yes, this is true.

Almost nobody in your class is willing to go the extra mile. Only 5 percent are willing to go outside of their comfort zone to do the work that is necessary. But when you do, you become a magnet and you attract into your life like-minded people who care about the very same things as you. This is when the most beautiful surprises begin to come your way. I am not asking you to believe me—try it and find out.

"Success is doing ordinary things extraordinarily well."

—Jim Rohn

~67~

How you go about personalizing the text, particularizing a specific moment, emotionally preparing, and other ways of bringing the character to life are nobody's business but yours. These acting elements are deeply personal and private. There is a power in keeping these things to yourself.

"The moment one gives close attention to anything, even a blade of grass, it becomes a mysterious, awesome, indescribably magnificent world in itself."

—Henry Miller

~68~

Here's one of my favorite things Sandy Meisner told us: "If you want to reach every person in the audience, it's not about being bigger, it's about going deeper."

"I regard the theatre as the greatest of all art forms, the most immediate way in which a human being can share with another the sense of what it is to be a human being."

—Oscar Wilde

~ **69** ~

There are days when you may want to give it all up. You may ask yourself, why bother working so hard and caring so much when many actors around you don't give a damn, winning accolades for their faking and posturing, rewarded for coming in unprepared, for being self-centered and self-ish, with no real interest in being a true collaborator or a trustworthy teammate. You may end up in an environment where not one person is willing to strive along with you to create a work of art, but rather, they are interested solely in impressing the critics.

So what do you do? As David Mamet says, if you are go-ing to continue to do what is necessary to be a true actor,

"You have not chosen it, it has chosen you," and there is no escape. If this is the situation you find yourself in, you must stay inspired, you must seek out sources of inspiration on a daily basis, you must be reminded that your work is necessary to the world and that you have the ability to alert people to the fact that they are not batteries to the machine. So, for today, I recommend a perfect reminder of why you are working so hard. It is a performance by a true master of the art of acting, Hal Holbrook. As with all great artists, he makes it look easy, like breathing. The film is That Evening Sun, and Mr. Holbrook was eighty-four when he made the film. Please see the film ASAP.

"Instead of art I have taught philosophy. Though technique for me is a big word, I never have taught how to paint. All my doing was to make people to see."

—Josef Albers

~70~

Today I want to talk about an important word when it comes to True Acting. The word is "stamina." Stamina is defined simply as the ability to sustain prolonged physical or mental effort. Endurance and fortitude are certainly necessary when you consider the great demands placed on you as a student of True Acting, and even more so as you enter the professional arena. I know for sure that most people who think about becoming an actor have no idea of the tremendous physical and emotional pressures they will have to withstand, and when confronted with these challenges, they are simply not prepared. Rehearsals of a play are exhausting and will require your complete physical and mental involvement for many hours each day, as will your performances eight times a week. Physically, an actor must be an athlete. I am not saying that you need to lift weights and run a marathon, but you have to be agile and flexible in your body and spirit, and you will need tremendous reserves of energy. More than you can imagine.

The tip? Have some sort of physical practice in your life. Find something that turns you on and feels good, like yoga or martial arts or jazz dance. Make it a ritual and integral to your life.

"Definiteness of purpose is the starting point of all achievement."

—W. Clement Stone

~71~

I love and admire True Actors; they are some of the most courageous people on the planet. Who else would purposely, night after night, and for very little financial return, venture into the dangerous realms of the unknown, relentlessly exploring the most volatile and core components of the human psyche, exposing their most intimate feelings and unguarded behavior to large groups of strangers who come to witness them at work?

"Let your performance do the thinking."

—Charlotte Brontë

One of the most destructive forces on the state of human relationships is something we call "beating around the bush." I am not really interested in exploring the reasons why so many people are unwilling to say the simple truth to another person, but I am interested in the ramifications—relationships that are dishonest, chaotic, decaying, or already dead. Since this is such a powerful and prevalent bad habit in life, of course we are going to see it dig in its claws in the acting classroom. Remember, acting is, in fact, an art of relationship.

One of the greatest gifts in the early training of True Actors is strengthening their ability to be "direct." The acting process reawakens the actors' ability to be the immediate expression of what is actually happening, saying exactly what they have to say rather than what they think they should say.

Think of it this way . . . The shortest distance between two points is a straight line. When you do not travel in a straight line, you create greater distance or, in other words, more space. Or think of a five-thousand-piece jigsaw puzzle; spill the pieces on a table and there is space between them. What you have is chaos. As you put the correct pieces together, you reduce the space between them, and suddenly, the puzzle starts to make sense. So, with less space, greater clarity and more beauty. This is also what we want in our communication—less space.

When we are direct, and communicating from our truthful point of view, the other person knows exactly what we mean, and in return, they can respond to this information from their own truthful point of view. Now we have two human beings in real contact with each other. We may not always like what the other person has to say, but when they are direct, they have given us a great gift, because now we know what we are dealing with and we can make decisions based on accurate information.

The great playwright David Mamet spoke to this when he said, "People still go to live theatre to be reminded that authentic communication between two human beings is still possible."

"No one saves us but ourselves. No one can and no one may. We ourselves must walk the path."

—Buddha

~73~

You must remember that, as an actor, the words are not your job; they are given to you by the playwright or the screenwriter. But for many actors, the words are their only concern—saying them beautifully, painting pictures with the words so the audience will be moved by the profound story they are telling, and making sure the words have the right inflection and tempo to keep the audience interested. All of this is done with the intent to trick the audience into believing that they really mean the things they are saying. Of course, the audience cannot be fooled. We call this kind of fakery "illustrating the words."

I want to impress upon you again that your job is about providing a river of life that the words can ride on. In the simplest terms, this means that you must make it personally necessary to speak those words.

"The difference between the right word and the almost right word is the difference between lightning and a lightning bug."

—Mark Twain

~74~

When you work on a role, you have to tackle the challenge from as many angles as possible, because you never know where the key to the lock of the "gate," the gate that stands between you and the character, will emerge from. You may find inspiration and greater clarity in a certain song, or in a painting, or you might get closer to the character's point of view in the eyes of a stranger at a coffee shop. Joanne Woodward once said that she found the character only when she would try on the right pair of shoes!

A few years back, I was in rehearsals for an off-Broadway production of an Athol Fugard play I was doing in New York City. One day, during our lunch break, I was picking up a few items at a CVS drug store on Ninth Avenue, down the street from our rehearsal studios. As I walked down one of the aisles, I was struck by a short, middle-aged woman who was picking some boxes of pain relievers off of the shelves. She caught my eye because of her very slow movements, and the way she held the box very, very close to her face. I stopped to watch from a distance, and I saw that she was wearing glasses with the thickest lenses I had ever seen. She would hold a box right up to one lens of the glasses, and it took her a long time to search the ingredients. Then she would have to put her face right against the shelf to find the place to put the box back. I watched her for quite a long time, doing the same thing with box after box. I also watched many people passing by her as if she weren't there in the aisle. One woman in very high heels bumped hard into her and kept going, not even stopping to see that she had knocked this little woman into the middle of the aisle, where she dropped a small paper bag she was carrying and became disoriented, reaching out to try and hold on to a shelf. As the paper bag fell to the floor, half of a sandwich wrapped in wax paper came out of the bag and ended up near her left foot. I went to her, picked up the paper bag, put the sandwich back in (noticing that it had two bites taken out of it), and offered her my hand. She raised her head and thanked me in an almost inaudible voice. I asked how I could help, and she quietly asked if I could find a certain box of pain relievers for her and if I would take her to the front register. While I did this, her fingers grasped my coat arm tightly; she was still shaking from the encounter with the high-heeled woman. As we walked together toward the front of the store, she moved silently and carefully and took little step by little step. When I got her to the register, she thanked me in a whisper and let go of my coat. And as I left the store, I turned one more time to see her holding a five-dollar bill right against the lens of her glasses.

When I got outside the store, I felt overcome with emotion, and down the street, I fell back against the wall of a building. In the play, I, too, wore thick glasses, was an outcast of society, and lived a "half sandwich in wax paper" kind of life. In the play, I, too, was someone who was mostly invisible to the rest of the world around me and forgotten by all family and human connections. In the play, I, too, would latch on to the coat arm of a stranger if only there were an arm to latch on to. This chance encounter with the woman in CVS unlocked a deeper understanding of everything I had been working on in relationship to the play and became a key to open that "gate" for me.

"That inner voice has both gentleness and clarity. So to get to authenticity, you really keep going down to the bone, to the honesty, and the inevitability of something."
—Meredith Monk

~75~

Coming soon!

When you work on a play or a film, you must make it the central focus of your life. It must become an obsession. Believe me, what you do in the rehearsal hall with the director and other actors is only a small portion of the work you must be doing. It is outside of the rehearsals where you take what you did that day and deepen it, make it your own, fantasize about it, and discover new approaches, objectives, and ideas that you will try out in your next rehearsal. You're tired? Who cares? Everyone working on the project is tired. Do your work. You need a break? When the run is over, you'll take a break. Do your work. Dig, dig, and dig some more. Care more than anyone else. Make sure that at the end of the run, the director comes to you and says, "You are the hardest-working actor I have ever worked with." This is the mark of the True Actor.

"What is art but a way of seeing?"

—Saul Bellow

~76~

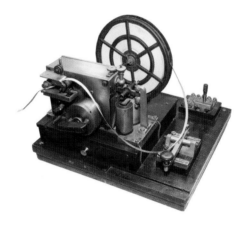

Here's something that many actors have great concerns about. There are many times when, in the middle of a scene, you will receive some sort of new information that will be extremely meaningful to the character you are playing. Very often, the text will make it clear that you need to have a strong emotional response to this information and, obviously, you cannot go off stage to emotionally prepare for this moment and you cannot ask the audience to wait while you turn your back to get into that emotional space. Yet you must fulfill the huge demands of this extreme event. So what do you do?

Have you heard the word "particularization"? This is a rehearsal technique that will help you with this challenging acting problem. Please underline the words "rehearsal technique," because if you try to stop and drum up the emotion during the play, you are no longer acting and you are no longer a part of the play at all.

Here's the first step into this thing called particularization. You need to ask yourself the "as if" question, which goes like this: "This moment in the play is 'as if' _____ were happening to me right now." Then, out of your imagination, based on an element of truth, you must fill in that blank. Did you notice that in the "as if" question, I included the words "right now"? Yes, that is a key. The other keys are "out of your imagination" and "an element of truth." Okay, ponder that a while, and in the next tip, I will dive deeper into this necessary acting skill.

> *"An artist is only an ordinary man*
> *with a greater potentiality—same stuff,*
> *same make up, only more force."*
>
> —D. H. Lawrence

~77~

Continuing on with "particularization."

Here's the moment in the play you need to particularize. You are playing a guy named Hal, who has been teaching part-time at the French Culinary Institute in New York City. Due to some anger-management issues, Hal has not worked as a chef in five years and, quite depressed, feels like his life is going nowhere. In the opening scene of act 2, Hal is in the midst of a heated argument with his mother when, suddenly, the phone rings. Hal grabs the phone and he gets the news that, out of ten candidates, he has been hired as the head chef at a new upscale French restaurant in SoHo. As Hal hangs up the phone, he has to say this line: "Yahoo, I'm back! I'm back! Thank you, God! I'm back!"

You have a challenge here. You, the actor, don't care at all about cooking. You don't care about French food, being a chef, or any of it. It all has no meaning to you whatsoever. But to say the words "Yahoo, I'm back! I'm back! Thank you, God! I'm back!" out of an authentic experience of triumph and joy, you have some inner work to do. Here's how. First, as we established in the previous tip, you must ask yourself this question: "This moment in the play is as if _____ were happening to me right now." Next, you must come up with an imaginary circumstance, based on an element of truth, that would bring you to that deep state of triumph and joy. The circumstance you create must be analogous to the needs of the scene. So you would come up with an imaginary situation in which you were suffering and hopeless and then, suddenly, you were given a new lease on life. Isn't that what has just happened with Hal? Let's continue the discussion in the next tip.

"Life is not complex. We are complex. Life is simple, and the simple thing is the right thing."

—Oscar Wilde

~78~

Particularization, part three.

In the previous tip, we established that you are playing a very down and depressed chef named Hal. And we know that at the beginning of act 2, Hal grabs the phone and gets the news that, out of ten candidates, he has been hired as the head chef at a new upscale French restaurant in SoHo. Hal hangs up the phone and he has to say this line: "Yahoo, I'm back! I'm back! Thank you, God! I'm back!" On my website, www.trueactinginstitute.com, I asked True Acting Tips readers to come up with an "as-if" to "particularize" this moment in the play. Here are three scenarios they submitted . . . Here's what Barbara sent in:

"The element of truth is that I actually married a man that my parents were very much against because he is a different religion then my whole family. My parents did not come to my wedding, and I have not spoken with them in four years. But I do get information about them from my younger sister. This has truly been the most painful thing in my life, and I still go to bed crying almost every night—I don't let my husband see. The imaginary part is that it is 'as if' I just got a call from my mother and she was crying and she asked me to forgive them for being so small-minded and that she misses me and she asked if I would come home to see them!"

Here's what Ariel sent in:

"I've been working a desk job doing accounting work (true story). I hate it!! Some days I utterly despise being there and dealing with everyone's attitude—clients calling up demanding that they be done by a certain time, blaming me for things that are out of my control, and the boss being demeaning and talking to me like I'm an idiot. I feel like a slave to my desk, money, and bills. So it is 'as if' I just got a call that I've received an inheritance from a family friend. The inheritance is set up in a perpetuity, which means I will receive $100,000 a year for the rest of my life! The day of reckoning has come, and I can finally tell my boss off and I can travel around the world like a gypsy. It's been a dream of mine to travel!"

Here's what Vinny sent in:

"I am in the hospital dying with cancer, and I just found out from my doctor that the chemo-therapy treatment beat the cancer and I'm going to live. Yahoo!!! I'm back, thank you, God!!! I'm back!!!!"

Thank you, Barbara, Ariel, and Vinny! Those are three very workable ways to personalize the meaning of the great news and fulfill the challenge of saying the words from the play out of an authentic experience of being overjoyed. The next question, then, is what do you do with the "as-if"?

In your rehearsal of this scene, when you get to the moment of hearing the good news on the telephone from the French restaurant, you would stop and close your eyes and do an emotional preparation based on your own "as-if." By emotional preparation, if you have not done one, I mean that you would have a free-association-type fantasy. Then, when the meaning of your imaginary circumstance "takes root," you would open your eyes and scream out the line from the play allowing it to "ride on" the wave of life created by your glorious fantasy. See how this works? But we are not done yet.

It would not be enough to do this one time; you would have to rehearse this moment over and over until the mean-ing of your imaginary circumstance actually lives inside the physical act of listening to the phone. What we are doing here is "Pavlovian (classical) conditioning." Pavlov rang the bell and the dogs would salivate. You listen to the phone and you are filled with joy. In this way, by the time you are reaching performance level, you will never have to think of your "as-if" again, because it will infiltrate the act of listening to the phone all on its own and you will be able to say, "Yahoo, I'm back! I'm back! Thank you, God! I'm back!" and actually mean it.

I want to be very clear here. The worst thing an actor can do is stop in the middle of a scene and try to drum up emotion. If you do this, your attention is on yourself and you are no longer in the play or with your partners onstage. (Believe me, working with this kind of actor is a most lonely and painful experience.) With the particularization, you never have to worry about the emotional result, because by leaving yourself alone in the most complete way and trusting the moment, the meaning will come up on its own without any effort at all.

"Genius is eternal patience."

—Michelangelo

~79~

The need to "look good" completely cripples your ability to function as an actor. I have seen many actors, in the midst of what are quite extreme circumstances in the scene, much more concerned with how their jeans are fitting and the condition of their hairdos. These actors are continually winking at the audience with the message, "Hey, it's just a play," and it's Tommy Hilfiger over Tennessee Williams every time. The process of True Acting frees you from these concerns so that you have the ability to follow the creative impulse wherever it leads you.

> "The quest for certainty blocks the search for meaning. Uncertainty is the very condition to impel man to unfold his powers."
>
> —Erich Fromm

~ 80 ~

In the previous tip, I introduced a guy we could have named "The Need to Look Good." Today I want you to meet his younger brother, "The Need to Be Appropriate." These guys work as a tag team, set on whittling you down to the least common denominator, until you become just like their first cousin, "Everyone Else." Now, let's not dismiss the value of knowing how to be appropriate in life. You may want to punch your boss in the mouth, but you resist the impulse, because keeping your job may be more important to you than knocking his teeth out. So, in this case, censoring your instinctual response was completely appropriate. But as an actor, you must learn how to give up the need to "be appropriate" so that you are free to become the spontane-ous expression of your impulses—as they are happening. When you do this, you are always appropriate to the needs of the moment.

"A bird does not sing because it has an answer; it sings because it has a song."

—Chinese proverb

~81~

Come to each day of rehearsal with a sense of play. Leap in, explore, investigate, improvise, lose your way and then find it again, make new discoveries, and play! Let's turn to the dictionary:

Play, a verb: "To engage in activity for enjoyment."

When I act, no matter where I have to go, physically and emotionally to bring the character to life, believe me, I am having the time of my life. There are moments of great suffering in the creative process, but for me, even that's fun! If it's not fun, you are in the wrong arena. And ultimately, if you're not having fun out on that stage, the audience is not having fun, either.

"The marvelous richness of human experience would lose something of rewarding joy if there were no limitations to overcome. The hilltop hour would not be half so wonderful if there were no dark valleys to traverse."

—Helen Keller

~82~

Just for today, give up all multitasking and attempt to give the next meal you eat your complete, undivided attention. How often do we eat meals in the midst of doing three other things so we don't even taste the food? For today, really taste the food. Attention is one of the vital steps on the path toward True Acting.

"If people knew how hard I worked to get my mastery, it wouldn't seem so wonderful at all."

—Michelangelo

~83~

Actors must read plays. Today, I urge you to get a hold of one of the greatest works of modern dramatic literature. It is called The Orphans Home Cycle, a series of nine plays (three parts, each with three plays) written by my friend and mentor Horton Foote.

"You have succeeded in life when all you really want is only what you really need."

—Vernon Howard

~84~

There is a wave of theater people who believe there is no such thing as "objectives" in dramatic literature and that the characters in these play are "objectiveless." Besides being inaccurate, this acting advice is also dangerous. It results in the most mushy, sentimental, purposeless kind of acting, actors aimlessly wandering around the stage, emotionally masturbating without any sense of what the play is about and why the character is there in the first place. Believe me, it is not a pretty sight. And not at all interesting.

Let's review. The truth of our lives is that from the time we get out of bed until the time we go back to sleep, we are continually involved in "objectives," things we are trying to accomplish. In every waking moment, conscious of this fact or not, we are behaving with purpose. If you take a hard look at your own life, you will see this is true. Now, some of these objectives might be fairly minor, like picking the soap up from the shower floor so that the next person does not slip and fall, or giving the waitress an extra-big smile when you ask for a "really hot" cup of coffee so that she makes sure the next cup is actually hot. Or your objective might be something major, like carefully choosing the engagement ring you are going to present to the woman whom you are about to propose to so she knows how in tune with her tastes you are, or getting the doctor to admit that he gave your mother less than adequate care, which resulted in her death.

Theater is like a microscope, and it zooms in on the fact that all behavior is purposeful in order to accomplish something. Also, acting technique must be related to how we operate as human beings, if it doesn't, it's false. In theater, we are reminded that the stakes are always high—we just forget. Objectives are the what keep you in the "channel" of the play and help you navigate the "oceans" of the script. Without them, you truly are lost at sea. Make sense?

Here's a related phrase that gets thrown around, "driving the objective." Hah! Let's talk about those three words in the next tip.

> "Three things cannot be long hidden:
> the sun, the moon, and the truth."
>
> —Buddha

~85~

I said I would address the phrase "driving the objective" in this tip. It is very easily understood. When there is true desire, you do not need to drive the objective; it will drive you.

Once again, we take this acting truth from our lives. Imagine you have a young child and suddenly the phone rings and it is the school nurse calling you with this news: "Your child took a very bad fall from the swings, and when the ambulance arrived she stopped breathing; they did emergency procedures and they are, right now, on the way to the hospital. Please go there to meet them at the emergency room."

My question to you is, are you going to get to the hospital? Will anything stop you? Your objective is very clear, yes? Now, do you need to drive the objective? Silly, right? Obviously, your strong desire to get to the hospital is going to drive you! It must be the same when you act. You must arrive at the place where you have the true desire to do the things you are doing. Then we have an actor who becomes like an arrow, always pointed at the target of his or her mission.

"Why shouldn't truth be stranger than fiction?
Fiction, after all, has to make sense."

—Mark Twain

~86~

As actors, you do not have a paintbrush, a canvas, and a palette of paints. So what are the colors you "paint" with? They spring from your "point of view"—how you see the world around you. Today I want to stress a point to consider . . .

As you work, you may encounter people who will have no qualms about trying to sway you from your truthful point of view and what is most important to you. Sometimes they do this simply for financial reasons and other times with more evil intentions. Stay alert! You must get very clear about what you are willing to say yes to and what you must say no to. If you abandon your truthful point of view, you literally have nothing left to work from. Don't you think there is a reason the struggle between Darth Vader and Luke Skywalker struck such a lasting and global chord? It is because all humans recognize it as true.

"Even if you are a minority of one, the truth is the truth."

—Gandhi

~87~

If your doctor lied to you about which medicine you need, would you be pleased? Is it okay for a chef to lie about the ingredients to the person who is eating the food? How would you feel if the electrician lied to you about the safety of the wires in your walls? So why should it be okay for an actor to lie to the audience? Listen, they paid a hundred dollars a ticket, they paid the babysitters, they spent another hundred on dinner, and they have been waiting for this special night for a month just to come and see the actors on the stage. Don't they deserve the real thing?

"A good head and a good heart are always a formidable combination."

—Nelson Mandela

~ 88 ~

By the time you reach opening night, if the director asks you at any moment in the rehearsal, "What are you doing right now?" you must to be able to answer specifically. If at any moment you are not able to answer that question specifically, you are not in the play, you are standing outside the play. To find your way back in, figure out what it is you are doing, and why you need to do it, and then really do it.

"By three methods we may learn wisdom: First, by reflection, which is noblest; Second, by imitation, which is easiest; and third by experience, which is the bitterest."

—Confucius

~89~

It's not the words you say, it's the music you play!

"He who devotes sixteen hours a day to hard study may become at sixty as wise as he thought himself at twenty."
—Mary Wilson Little

~90~

One of the hardest parts of being an actor is that because it is a collaborative art; you have to do it with other people, and there may not always be a daily opportunity to do what you most love to do. In this way, it is very different from being a painter who can sit alone in his room and paint. So there may be times when you question yourself: "I am not really doing anything—am I really an actor at all?" The trap is to sit back and wait for somebody to give you a job. Here, your negative inner voices may get stronger, saying, "I am not an actor, I am just not an actor."

Vincent Van Gogh said, "If you hear a voice within you say, 'You cannot paint,' then by all means paint and that voice will be silenced."

I urge you to make your own work. Find groups of like-minded people and create projects together. Find a space and mount an evening of scenes or one-act plays. Do your best to stay active and see where it leads.

"Judge each day not by the harvest you reap but by the seeds you plant."

—Robert Louis Stevenson

The question is "What gets you out of bed each morning?"

The answer is "Desire." Let's explore this together. I have a new distinction for you. It is not that we have desire—and we do have desire—it is that we are desire. Read this again very carefully:

It is not that we have desire—and we do have desire—it is that we are desire.

This may sound a little odd to you, but I want you to give it some thought. What might I mean by "We are desire?" Think of it this way, what got Mommy and Daddy together in the first place? Desire. You know, that fateful day at the grocery store, when Daddy got his first look at your mom, dropped the tomatoes, and said to himself, Wow!" And Mommy got her first look back at your dad, dropped the lettuce, and said to herself, Wow!" Suddenly, Mommy and Daddy were making salad together. And what do you think led to their first kiss? Desire. And then, of course, we get to you. You began in the midst of some real strong desire, don't you think?

Of course, if we look at the story of the sperm and the egg, we are looking at the clearest factual and scientific evidence that we are desire. Out of millions, how many sperm fulfill their ultimate quest? Yes, one. And that's no easy journey the sperm sets out on. The environment it finds itself in has huge obstacles in store. But does that determined little guy cave in to these pressures?

So, you see, on a cellular level, you and I, all of us, are desire, and we cannot elude the power of its force on our lives. Yes, some people try to evade the power of desire. But think about this interesting fact. Isn't it true that the person who has committed himself to the effort to give up all desire, by seeking a guru on the mountaintop, has merely adopted the "desire to have no desire?" The answer, of course, is yes. You see? More desire.

If you stop to examine it, you will find that behind every choice you make, underneath every word you speak, inside every thought you think, fueling every fantasy you imagine, and even infiltrating your dreams is desire! It's there in the things that run around in your mind before you fall asleep at night, and it's there in the morning when you awake, driving you out of your bed. (Along with having to go to the bathroom.)

Why is this so important to come to terms with? Why is it so vital to see the effects of desire in your own life? It is important because every character you will ever play is also a human being who is living with a specific and unquenchable desire. Ultimately, if you cannot understand the desire of the character in both a human and deeply personal way, you cannot play the part.

Next . . .

As soon as there is desire, there is another force in our lives that comes into play. It is just as powerful and just as real. Let's get into that conversation in the next tip.

"Man never made any material as
resilient as the human spirit."

—Bern Williams

~92~

In the previous tip, we explored desire as a deep and constant human component, and I told you that now, we would discuss another force in our lives that is just as powerful and just as real. Consider this:

As soon as there is desire—and I stated that "we are desire"—there will be a force that opposes this desire. This is always true. Always.

I call this force "the opponent."

You can count on the fact that the opponent will be present to make it more difficult to accomplish the things you desire. You may not prefer it, like it, or believe it, but when you look at life with eyes really open, you see that this is the way life is built. To get more specific, there are two types of opponents we are faced with. In this tip, I will investigate with you "the external opponent."

Every day, all people, including you and I, go about their lives with their own deeply held desires. Sometimes, an outside force will step in and make fulfilling that desire very challenging or attempt to wipe out the desire all together. Here's a simple example of an external opponent.

Shelley has just moved to New York City, and she found a job waitressing at a hotel coffee shop. She is twenty-one, just out of a college acting program, and plans to start acting classes when she saves up enough money. After two months of working at the coffee shop, Shelley has had a difficult time making friends, but last week, something wonderful happened. Shelley was invited by Carol, another aspiring actress and the coffee shop manager, to hang out at Carol's apartment after work.

Carol and Shelley had a great time during that first visit, and they began to get together every day after work to practice monologues, read the trade papers, et cetera.

On a few of the visits, Carol's best friend, Stacey, also came over. Stacey has not said anything to Carol, but she is very jealous and she is not happy that Carol has been spending time with Shelley.

Today, Stacey told a lie to Carol. She told Carol that she heard Shelley talking to another waitress at work and that Shelley told this person that Carol is not very talented and should really give up all hope of being an actress. Stacey knows that Carol has great fears about spending the rest of her life as a coffee shop manager and is very insecure about her own acting skills.

Carol was very upset to hear that Shelley had betrayed their new friendship. So, although they were supposed to get together again today, Carol just told Shelley that she had to cancel their get-together and that she is going to be too busy to get together next week, as well.

My question for you is, who is the "external opponent" in this little story? And what desires did the opponent step in to attempt to destroy?

If you said that Stacey is the external opponent, you are correct. Do you see how both Carol and Shelley had very simple desires that brought them together, and how Stacey stepped in to try to wipe out these desires? What were the desires Stacey could not tolerate?

Shelley had the deep desire to make a friend. Carol also had a desire to make a new friend and to be with someone who was fun to hang out with. But Stacey, acting out of a place of fear and a self-serving, selfish attitude, wreaked havoc on the new bond forming between Shelley and Carol. She also caused a lot of pain, right? Yes, the external opponent always causes pain.

Here is an interesting example to highlight the basic truth of the force called "the opponent." It's called sports. Obvious, right? Yes, all sports were created to have a specific desire and an opponent who makes the desire more difficult to accomplish. And who created sports? People did. People created sports as a reflection of the truth of our lives, and they intensified this truth and raised the stakes. Hey, that's just like theater!

Let's look at football for a moment. If you are on the New York Jets team and you have the ball at your own five-yard line, how many yards do you need to go to get a touchdown? Yes, you need to go another ninety-five yards. Isn't that your desire, to get a touchdown? Yes, it is. So, with the football on your own five-yard line, will the other team, the Miami Dolphins—your opponent—try to stop you from making progress in your effort? Yes, they will.

Now imagine that you have moved the ball forward ninety yards and you are on the Dolphins' five-yard line, with only have to go five yards to score the touchdown. My question is, here on their five-yard line, will the Dolphins' defense get less intense or more intense? Yes, more intense! And this is how the opponent operates in our lives, as well. The closer we get to fulfilling our desire, the more fierce the opponent will become.

Writing assignments . . .

Of course, you will also find this life truth in every great movie or play. In your journal, consider and write about Lord of the Rings. When Frodo takes on the mission of the ring, what is his desire? Does he face any opponents? Who are they? Does Frodo suffer? How about Romeo and Juliet? What is the desire of the young lovers? Who are the opponents? Do Romeo and Juliet suffer?

Here are some more writing assignments for your

journal work. First, I want you to write about examples of the external opponent from history. What events have you studied that are clear instances of the external opponent, in his lust for power, destroying the desires of other people in the world?

Next, please write about times when you have encountered the external opponent in your own life. Get specific. What was your desire, and how did the opponent try to sabotage it? Did that person succeed? Did this cause you pain?

See if you can identify any times in your life when, unfortunately, you may have done something that made you the external opponent in someone else's life and you caused them pain. It might be as simple as a time when your little brother wanted that last chocolate chip cookie and you took it out of his hand and ate it yourself.

Go ahead and write and see what you come up with: identify when you have had an external opponent squashing your desire and when you have been the external opponent to someone else.

As I said at the beginning of this tip, we face two kinds of opponents in life. In the next tip, we will get to part two of the story.

"Your present circumstances don't determine where you can go; they merely determine where you start."

—Nido Qubein

In the previous tip, we discussed "the opponent," and I told you that there are two manifestations of this force in our lives. We addressed the external form of the opponent and I promised that in this tip, we would get to the second part of the story. By the way, do you have any idea why I am spending so much time on this topic? It is because these forces are also present in every script you will ever read, and having a clear grasp on how these human qualities show up in your own life is a key to inhabiting the characters you will be playing.

The Internal Opponent

The truth is that we often create our own obstacles to fulfilling our deepest desires. Do you know about Ed, the construction worker who had a peanut butter and jelly sandwich for lunch every day?

Every day, when the horn blew at 12:00, Ed would sit with the other guys on the crew, open his lunch box, and pull out a sandwich. As he unwrapped the sandwich and saw that it was peanut butter and jelly, Ed would cry out, "I hate peanut butter and jelly sandwiches!" This went on for months and months. Every single day Ed would open his lunch box, pull out his sandwich, unwrap it, see the peanut butter and jelly, and cry out, "I hate peanut butter and jelly sandwiches!" Finally, Bob, who sat next to Ed every day, yelled back, "Man! Why don't you tell your wife to make you a different sandwich!" Ed screamed back, "What wife? I'm single—I make my own sandwiches!"

To begin to make clear to you the "internal opponent," here's a question. Have you ever had the experience, maybe late at night when you are in your room by yourself, of your mind being flooded with thoughts and usually the thoughts aren't so pleasant? And no matter what you do, the thoughts will not stop? Maybe the thoughts sound like this: "What's the matter with me?" or, "I'm not good enough!" or, "I'll never be as good as so and so!" or, "I'm just too dumb to ever succeed!" and on and on.

I have asked this same question to groups I have worked with in every part of the world, all across Europe, South America, Canada, and the United States. In every group, no matter what language they speak, every hand in the room goes up with people saying, "Yes, I have these kinds of thoughts." Isn't that interesting? Isn't it interesting that people all around the world are having the same, uncontrollable, self-critical thoughts as you?

Well, if that's the case, then let's suppose for a moment that the thoughts aren't even your own. Let's imagine that instead of the thoughts coming from your own mind, there is a radio station with a powerful transmitter and it has a very tall antenna. Let's imagine that the radio station is pumping out all of these negative thoughts and you have simply tuned in to this station. You didn't mean to tune in, but somehow, you and every other person all around the world did tune in, and all of you are pulling in these negative thoughts from the airwaves.

Here's my next question. Does an infant have these kinds of negative, self-critical thoughts? If you are an infant and your mommy is pushing you in your stroller, and another baby goes by in her stroller and she is wearing the expensive diapers, do you think that you would have a thought like, "Hey! That baby has the good diapers! Why didn't my mommy get me the good diapers? This sucks! I knew it, my mommy really doesn't love me!" Or if the other baby going by had curly hair, do you think you would have thoughts like, "Why didn't I get curly hair? My hair is straight—I am so plain, no one will ever like me!" Do you think a little baby has these kinds of thoughts? Obviously not, right?

So, if you did not have these thoughts when you were born, when did you tune in to the "critical thought radio station"? Was it when you started to go to school? Was it when your parents first scolded you? Was it when you first began to play with other kids and you compared yourself to them? Well, scientists have some ideas about all of this, but the truth is that we don't really know precisely when these negative thoughts begin to take control of the mind. The important thing to take note of from this new awareness has to do with "attention."

Here's a simple question. When you are listening to the thoughts in your mind, where is your attention? Is it directed out toward the world around you, or is it directed inward toward yourself? Yes, obviously, if you are listening to the thinking in your head, your attention is directed at yourself. This means that in these periods of time when you are absorbed in the negative thinking, you are no longer available to the world around you. This is a problem in two main respects. First, life and aliveness is accessible to us only when we are in relationship with the world around us in the present moment. Second, when your attention is more on yourself than on what is happening around you, you are in danger! I am sure you have heard the saying, "Lost in thought."

Here's a story about the danger of being lost in thought. When I was very young and I was living in New York City, I was on the corner of 57th Street and Ninth Avenue at 7:00 a.m., waiting for a bus. I was eating a banana and I was lost in thought. Did you ever see in the cartoons where the character gets hit in the head and he sees stars? Well, I was eating my banana, lost in thought, and suddenly something hit me so hard on my forehead that I literally saw stars! I went reeling back, but I stayed on my feet. When my eyes finally opened, I saw a crazy-looking man with wild, knotted hair, about twenty feet away from me holding a big two-by-four piece of wood and waving it in the air. That big piece of wood was what had just bashed me in the head. I remember the two of us, the crazy man and I, staring each other in the eyes. He looked like he was going to come at me again with that wood at any moment. And then, just as suddenly as I was hit, the guy turned and ran off and disappeared into the traffic. At the same time, the bus pulled up in front of me. I climbed up the stairs of the bus, dropped in some money, sat in an empty seat, and finished eating my banana, which was still in my hand!

For months and months after that incident, I suffered from a severe concussion and all of the symptoms that go with it. What a wake-up call, don't you think? Yes, it was. It was a big lesson in the importance of being awake and the danger of walking through life lost in thought.

Now let's talk about babies again. Have you been around them much? Well, if you have, you can see that they always have their attention where? Yes, at all times, babies have their attention directed out toward the world around them. When you play with a baby, or make silly faces at them, you know that their total attention is on you. I think this is one of the reasons why almost everyone in the world loves being with babies. They remind us that we are, in fact, human beings. (And this is exactly what great theater offers. Great theater reminds the audience that they are human.)

Then the baby grows up and, unfortunately, like most people, puts a mirror up in front of his or her face. Think about this for a moment. I just said that most people in this world are walking around with a mirror up in front of their face. For these people, their attention goes out toward the mirror and bounces back onto themselves. And with their attention on themselves, the self-critical and negative thinking gets more intense. That radio station we discussed earlier gets louder and louder. "What do people think about me?" "How do I look?" "No one will ever love me!" This, in fact, is the "internal opponent," and, just like the external opponent, the internal opponent causes great suffering. Have you experienced this yourself?

Here's the good news. First, because you were once a baby, you already have the ability to live without listening to the radio station, but it will take some work to retrain yourself. In fact, the Meisner approach offers an effective way to reawaken and strengthen your innate ability to have your attention directed out toward the world so that you are no longer plagued by the control mechanisms of the mind. What a relief. It is also the jumping-off place for this thing I call True Acting.

"But what is happiness except the simple harmony
between a man and the life he leads?"

—Albert Camus

Hard work pays off

The cornerstone, the bedrock, the backbone of True Acting is "working hard," and this is why I have always told students upfront that this approach is not for everyone. I do believe that anyone who is willing to do the unrelenting work that needs to be done will make progress beyond anything they could have possibly imagined. But this concept is not unique to the art of acting, Vidal Sassoon said,

"The only place where success becomes before work is in the dictionary."

Garson Kanin said,

"Amateurs hope. Professionals work."

Confucius said,

"The expectations of life depend upon diligence; the

mechanic that would perfect his work must first sharpen his tools."

Find these thoughts appetizing? Great, get to work.

"A man sooner or later discovers that he is the master-gardener of his soul, the director of his life."

—James Allen

For your pleasure and for consideration, a folk tale . . .

How One Little Feather Became Five Hens

"That is a terrible story!" said a Hen in a quarter of the town where the affair had not happened. "That is a terrible story from a poultry-yard. I dare not sleep alone to-night! It is quite fortunate that there are so many of us on the roost together!" And she told a tale, which made the feathers of the other hens stand on end, and the cock's comb fall down flat. It is quite true!

But we will begin at the beginning; and that took place in a poultry-yard in another part of the town. The sun went down, and the fowls jumped up on their perch to roost. There was a Hen, with white feathers and short legs, who laid eggs regularly and was a respectable hen in every way; as she flew up on to the roost she pecked herself with her beak, and a little feather fell from her.

"There it goes!" said she; "the more I peck myself, the handsomer I grow!" And she said it quite merrily, for she was a joker among the hens, though, as I have said, she was very respectable; and then she went to sleep.

It was dark all around; the hens sat side by side on the roost, but the one that sat next to the merry Hen did not sleep: she heard and she didn't hear, as one should do in this world if one wishes to live in peace; but she could not help telling it to her neighbor.

"Did you hear what was said here just now? I name no names; but here is a hen who wants to peck her feathers out to look well. If I were a cock I should despise her."

And just above the hens sat the Owl, with her husband and her children; the family had sharp ears, and they all heard every word that the neighboring Hen had spoken. They rolled their eyes, and the Mother-Owl clapped her wings and said,

"Don't listen to it! But I suppose you heard what was said there? I heard it with my own ears, and one must hear much before one's ears fall off. There is one among the fowls who has so completely forgotten what is becoming conduct in a hen that she pulls out all her feathers, while the cock sits looking at her."

"Think of the children," said the Father-Owl. "That's not a story for them to hear."

"I'll tell it to the neighbor owl; she's a very proper owl to associate with." And she flew away.

"Hoo! hoo! to-whoo!" they both screeched in front of the neighbor's dovecote to the doves within. "Have you heard it? Have you heard it? Hoo! hoo! there's a hen who has pulled out all her feathers for the sake of the cock. She'll die with cold, if she's not dead already."

"Coo! coo! Where, where?" cried the Pigeons.

"In the neighbor's poultry-yard. I've as good as seen it myself. It's hardly proper to repeat the story, but it's quite true!"

"Believe it! Believe every single word of it!" cooed the Pigeons, and they cooed down into their own poultry-yard. "There's a hen, and some say that there are two of them that have plucked out all their feathers, that they may not look like the rest, and that they may attract the cock's attention. That's a dangerous thing to do, for one may catch cold and die of a fever, and they are both dead."

"Wake up! wake up!" crowed the Cock, and he flew up on to the plank; his eyes were still heavy with sleep, but yet he crowed. "Three hens have died of a broken heart. They have plucked out all their feathers. That's a terrible story. I won't keep it to myself; pass it on."

"Pass it on!" piped the Bats; and the fowls clucked and the cocks crowed, "Pass it on! Pass it on!" And so the story traveled from poultry-yard to poultry-yard, and at last came back to the place from which it had gone forth.

"Five fowls," it was told, "have plucked out all their feathers to show which of them had become thinnest out of love to the cock; and then they have pecked each other, and fallen down dead, to the shame and disgrace of their families, and to the great loss of their master."

And the Hen who had lost the little loose feather of course did not know her own story again; and as she was a very respectable Hen, she said, "I despise those hens; but there are many of that sort. One ought not to hush up such a thing, and I shall do what I can that the story may get into the papers, and then it will be spread over all the country, and that will serve those hens right, and their families, too."

It was put into the newspaper; it was printed.
And it's quite true—that one little feather may
easily become five hens.

"In everyone's life, at some time, our inner fire goes
out. It is then burst into flame by an encounter with
another human being. We should all be thankful
for those people who rekindle the inner spirit."

—Albert Schweitzer

If a cat is onstage, playing with a ball of yarn, every eye in the audience will be glued to the cat. Why? Because the cat has what we call "presence."

One definition for the word "presence" is, "The quality of certain performers that enables them to achieve a rapport with and hold the attention of their audiences."

What are the True Acting values that explain the cat's presence and why he commands the audience's attention? Look at the next tip.

"Lose not yourself in a far off time,
seize the moment that is thine."

—Friedrich Schiller

The question from the previous tip was, "What True Acting values explain a cat's presence onstage, and why does he command the attention of the audience?" True Acting Tips readers had this to say . . .

Brittany in Nebraska said, "A cat is always living moment by moment without any thought of the future or the past." Yes, Brittany, great! Reminds me of an old joke, "Did you ever know a dog who was late?" (Why is it that every time I tell that joke in class, I am the only one laughing? Very frustrating.) Also, can you imagine a cat onstage thinking, "Damn, I did this yarn scene much better last night!" Or "Man, if they like this yarn bit, wait until they see my next scene where I wrestle with the toy mouse!" Crazy, right? Only bad actors have these kind of thoughts. Cats? Never.

Alexandre in Paris sent this reply: "The cat plays with the yarn completely. When he is involved with the yarn, the yarn is his whole world for that period of time, until something else demands his attention, and then that thing becomes his whole world." Alexandre, fantastic response! Yes, we call this "Fully doing what you are doing." And as Sandy Meisner said, "The quality of your acting depends on how fully you do what you are doing." That means, whatever you do, you must give it one hundred percent of your attention. Then, when your attention is pulled to something else, you must give that thing one hundred percent of your attention. Take a look at your life and you will see how rare it is that we do anything fully. We are on the computer, while talking on the phone, while eating a bowl of chips, while changing our socks, while pouring a glass of juice, and on and on, doing many things partially and doing nothing fully. People texting while driving—horrifying!

Misha from Bucharest sent in this comment: "The cat is actually playing with the yarn. What I mean is, he is actually involved and not pretending to be involved." Misha, very cool! You hit on another great True Acting value, which we call "The Reality of Doing." This means that when we do something, we actually do it. We don't pretend; we don't fake; and we don't try to make it look like we are doing it. Many actors try to make it look like something is happening when nothing is happening. We call this "indicating," and it is the polar opposite of everything we are after in our True Actor training.

"Leap, and the net will appear."

—John Burroughs

There is a zen story about a man who studied with a master for a while and told the master, "I want the truth." And the master said, "Cut trees for a while." So the student cut trees for a year. Finally he reminded the master, "I've been asking you for the truth." The master replied, "Go out and turn all those trees into charcoal." So the student did that for six months, and the master never spoke to him. Finally, the young man said, "Listen, master, I am leaving you. I told you I wanted the truth." The master said, "Let me walk with you a way."

They walked together until they came to a bridge and stepped onto it. Under it, there was rushing water. The master gave the student a shove, sending him into the water. The man slipped under the surface. "I can't swim!" he cried. Down again, "I can't swim!" The third time, the master pulled him up onto the bridge and said, "Now, when you want truth the same way you wanted that breath of air, you've already got it."

"Because things are the way they are, things
will not stay the way they are."

—Bertolt Brecht

~99~

As an artist of the theater, from the classroom to the stage, you are continually putting yourself in the position of being critiqued. How do you handle criticism? David Mamet suggested that actors be like plumbers when it comes to having their work judged by others. He said that if a plumber is told that the pipes he just repaired are still leaking, the plumber isn't going to break down and cry—he will just go back and fix the pipes. Well, this is great as a concept, but the truth is, we are not plumbers and we are not working with pipes. At the same time, if you do need the approval of anyone—teacher, audience, or critic—you have become their prisoner. So, my friend, the question for today is, how will you set yourself free so you can function fully?

> "Everything has been said before, but since nobody listens we have to keep going back and beginning all over again."
>
> —André Gide

~100~

Last night, I was coming out from an electronics store. As I walked into the parking lot, I noticed a man, about seventy-five years old, leaning back, collapsed against an open door of his Ford Taurus station wagon, and gripping his head in his hands. The engine was running, all the doors of the car were open, and on the ground, all around the car, were books, clothing, empty potato chip bags, crushed soda cups from Wendy's, jump wires, tools, and lots of other items the man had obviously taken out of the car. As I got closer, the man turned as his knees buckled, and he grabbed on to the car door for support. I ran over to him, helped him stand, and he yelled out an angry, "It sucks getting old!" When he was stable on his feet, I asked if him if there was any way I could help. Very upset, he said, "My wife is in the hospital. They don't think she's going to make it. She asked me to come to her office to get a photo she keeps on her desk of our daughter, our daughter when she was four years old. I had the photo, I had it right here in the car, and then it was gone. Where the hell is it? She wants to see her curly hair one more time, just one more time." At this point, he was sobbing and gripping my shoulder and saying, "I gotta get back to the hospital, I gotta get back there!" I told him I would help him find the picture. His knees gave out again, and I helped him sit in the car. I quickly went carefully through each item on the ground, and fortunately, as I picked up one of those soda cups from Wendy's, I found the photo stuck to the bottom of the wet cup. When I handed it to him, he screamed out, "Oh my, oh my, thank you, thank you," and he cried even harder this time. I told him that he really shouldn't be driving and offered to take him to the hospital. We left everything on the ground as I helped him over to my car, and he held the photo very tightly in his right hand as we drove to the hospital.

How does this experience I have shared relate to this thing called True Acting, which we have been exploring together here in the tips? What acting elements do you see present in this life event?

"Life is the art of drawing without an eraser."

—John Gardner

~101~

Here is a response to the question raised in the previous tip, submitted by Chelsy in Florida:

What a touching . . . heartbreaking . . . uplifting story. This man has such an extreme circumstance he's experiencing with his wife dying in the hospital. I can imagine they have been together much longer than I have even been alive. His partner, his best friend, his soul mate, requesting something of utmost importance of him. His truth is so clear to him that he must accomplish this task. He probably felt relief when he found the picture at his wife's office, only to be sideswiped when the picture had gone missing.

Now, no matter how physically difficult this task is, he must find this picture to give to his wife of their daughter when she was four years old. As the person coming into this scene, you are drawn in by a very human pull of love and empathy for this elderly man. What the man must have thought to have someone step up and not only help him accomplish this task, that in a sense is completely joyous when achieved, but to take the time and patience to drive him to the hospital and complete what he has set out to do.

"The seat of knowledge is in the head,
of wisdom, in the heart."

—William Hazlitt

~102~

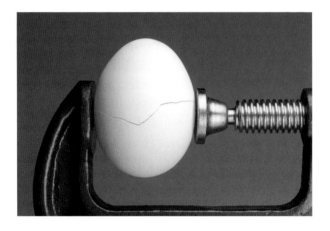

When a production is mounted at any level, there is pressure on everyone involved. Of course, professional productions have intense additional strain with the risk of losing great amounts of money and not coming through for the investors. So, there are tremendous concerns from the get-go about getting great results. Of course, these early concerns about the ultimate results, and succeeding financially, can totally cripple the very creative process that would lead to success. Sometimes, producers will come and sit in on rehearsals and, without any real understanding of acting, directing, or anything to do with the actual work at hand, will call a meeting with the director and try to change things for their own misguided reasons. I love something Harold Clurman said about the rehearsals of a play:

"Rehearsals of a play constitute a creative process as delicate and arduous as the writing of the script itself. The process is not helped, it is impeded, by nervous impatience or the insistence on immediately convincing results. These are the fruits of gestation. While this is going on, what we see is rarely pleasing as 'performance.' Only the late stages of rehearsal provide testimony to the progress made."

"The ultimate measure of a man is not where he stands in moments of comfort, but where he stands at times of challenge and controversy."
—Martin Luther King Jr.

~103~

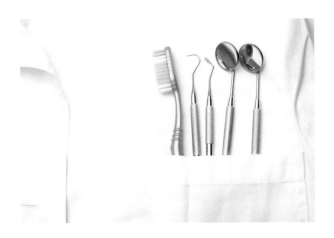

I was at the dentist's office today with my son. Next to me sat a mom, busy reading a travel magazine while her four-year-old daughter was making friends with an elderly woman who sat across from them, waiting to have her teeth cleaned. Soon, the little girl got her hands on the woman's handbag and she started to take out everything that was inside, piling it all up on the floor. The elderly woman had a tight smile on her face, but she never stopped the little girl, and the mother was too involved in an article on the fifty best beaches in the world to notice the action. The last thing to come out of the bag was some lipstick, which the little girl twisted open. She climbed onto the woman's lap and started to apply the pale pink wax to the woman's lips. The elderly woman was not happy about this, and she cleared her throat loudly, gaining the attention of the little girl's mom. The little girl turned to her mother, and I saw them make connection with their eyes. Not a word was said and not a muscle in the mother's face altered in any way, but immediately, the little girl closed up the lipstick, climbed down from the woman's lap, and proceeded to put all of the stuff on the floor back into the handbag.

Have you heard the expression, "To have your child's eye"? What this refers to is the intimate connection that exists between two people who are very close and who communicate without words or any external behavior whatsoever. This is what happened between the mother and daughter at the dentist's office. The instant the two of them made eye contact, the mother sent the message "Cut it out or else!" and the little girl responded. This kind of intimate availability to another human being is also the aim of True Acting.

"Storms make oaks take roots."

—Proverb

~104~

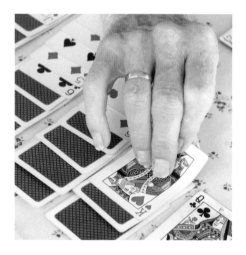

Today, a young actress asked if I thought it was a good idea to stay "in character" when you are in a play and you are not out onstage. My very short answer was, "Yes." Listen, this is not "method acting" advice, it's simply creative, fun, and imaginative and will help you with knowing where you are coming from when you enter into your next scene. Hey, come' on, the performance is under two hours long—why not invest yourself fully and create a whole world that feeds you and incites you to take action? Doesn't this sound more productive than playing solitaire?

"We are all inventors, each sailing out on a voyage of discovery, guided each by a private chart, of which there is no duplicate. The world is all gates, all opportunities."

—Ralph Waldo Emerson

~105~

When you play a character who behaves badly, the worst possible choice is to play the role with negative intent. You must always think of these characters in positive terms because, the truth is, all people justify their behavior. So when playing a villain, always see your character as a person acting with the best intentions for their own, very specific reasons.

"You cannot plough a field by turning it over in your mind."

—Author unknown

~106~

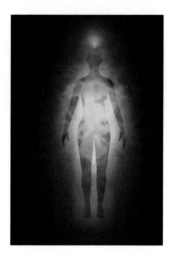

I do believe that for True Actors, acting is a profoundly spiritual event, as they are calling on the deeper voice that has been planted in each one of us from the original spark of life. The truth is that we do not have to look outside ourselves to play the character, because we already have the "knowing" of the particular point of view that the character embodies; it is already in our DNA, handed down to us through the experiences of our ancestors and from the beginning of time. Ahh, but how to call it forth, how to tap into that specific voice.

This is where we approach the mysterious and unexplainable, which is the goal of True Actor training, putting us on the path toward that gate and giving us the way in. The specific medium of any art is nothing more than a sensitive membrane that encases the mysterious. With great theater, not only does the audience experience the production through their physical senses, they are more deeply affected by the force of life that vibrates inside it.

Albert Einstein expressed this in the most eloquent way when he was once asked if he was, in fact, religious. He replied:

"Yes, you can call it that. Try and penetrate with our limited means the secrets of nature and you will find that, behind all the discernible laws and connections, there remains something subtle, intangible, and inexplicable. Veneration for this force beyond anything that we can comprehend is my religion. To that extent I am, in fact, religious."

"If the wind will not serve, take to the oars."

—Latin proverb

~107~

I want to build on the previous tip with another gift from Albert Einstein. In 1930, Einstein published a credo he called "What I Believe." It concluded with an explanation of what he meant when he called himself religious. I like to think that Einstein was sending a wake-up call to the sleeping, though I doubt his critics, who were so focused on the argument of whether Einstein believed in God or not, even noticed. Here is what he wrote:

"The most beautiful emotion we can experience is the mysterious. It is the fundamental emotion that stands at the cradle of all true art and science. He to whom this emotion is a stranger, who can no longer wonder and stand rapt in awe, is as good as dead, a snuffed-out candle. To sense that behind anything that can be experienced there is something that our minds cannot grasp, whose beauty and sublimity reaches us only indirectly: this is religiousness. In this sense, and this sense only, I am a devoutly religious man."

"If you would create something, you must be something."

—Goethe

~108~

True Actors have refined their craft to the point where they are not solely dependent on the director to fulfill the needs of the production. In the best working conditions, actors are, in fact, contributors to how the play is being directed.

You must be strong on your own two feet as an actor, because the truth is, many directors do not have an intimate understanding of the acting process and they will not be able to help you. So, when the director asks you to produce a certain result, it will be up to you to fulfill that demand authentically. I am not saying that all directors will be interested in an authentic response, but I hope it will be vitally important to you. No matter what the forces around you may be, you must know how to do the work, and then you must do it.

Harold Clurman, the great director and founder of the Group Theatre, said:

"Too great a dependence on the director is unhealthy for both actor and play."

Good directors are collaborators, and though they must ultimately be the guiding force that shapes every element that is witnessed by the audience, the collaborative director will instigate the actors to bring forth all that they are and everything they imagine, feel, and can create. This pursuit will open up doors that the director did not know existed. Together, the director and the actors are building something piece by piece. Peter Brook gave my favorite description of a good director: "A real director is someone who climbs down into the pit with the actors and, somehow, together, they all claw their way out."

"I cannot give you the formula for success,
but I can give you the formula for failure,
which is: Try to please everybody."

—Herbert Bayard Swope

~109~

Have you ever met a brand-new person and found that suddenly, right after you tell them your name, they talk for fifteen minutes, without taking a breath, about their most private issues and problems? Did you ever meet a new person and find your own behavior surprising or frustrating or unexpected?

When you take a look at it, life is a series of introductions; we are continually introducing ourselves to other people, and other people are continually introducing themselves to us.

I have two useful exercises for you that are related to the understanding of the acting element we call "character."

For the next week, I want you to examine two sides of the same coin. First, after each time you encounter and engage with someone new in the world—it might be a waitress, a taxi driver, a friend of a friend, a new co-worker—I want you to stop and ask yourself, "What was I just trying to accomplish with this person?" Be absolutely honest with yourself and write down your response to this question in your journal. Next, ask the same question, but now related to the other person: "What was he or she just trying to accomplish with me?" See if you have a sense of what it is. You may feel uncertain, but see what your instinct tells you about the reason for the other person's behavior, which includes their physical actions as well as the words they spoke to you and what they chose not to say.

These two experiments lead to a very clear understanding that we are, in every moment, trying to accomplish something specific, and the key word here is "specific." The same is true for the character in the play. So see it and feel it in your life, and then bring this life truth to your acting.

"The great blessings of mankind are within us and within our reach; but we shut our eyes, and like people in the dark, we fall foul upon the very thing we search for, without finding it."

—Seneca

~110~

Minnie Maddern Fiske, also known as "Mrs. Fiske," was called by many the most important American stage actress at the beginning of the twentieth century. She had many insightful things to say about acting and important advice for the young actor. (As you read the following, note that when she talks about "science," she is really referring to the training of the actor as an artist.)

Here for your pleasure, some words from Mrs. Fiske . . .

I like to remind myself that there can be, that there is, a complete technique of acting. Great acting, of course, is a thing of the spirit; in its best state is a conveyance of certain abstract spiritual qualities, with the person of the actor as medium. It is with this medium our science deals, with its slow, patient perfection as an instrument. The eternal and immeasurable accident of the theater which you call genius, that is a matter of the soul.

But with every genius I have seen, there was always the last word in technical proficiency. The inborn, mysterious something in these players can only inspire. It cannot be imitated. No school can make a Duse. But with such genius as hers has always gone a supreme mastery of the science of acting, a precision of performance so satisfying that it continually renews our hope and belief that acting can be taught. Any one may achieve on some rare occasion an outburst of genuine feeling, a gesture of imperishable beauty, a ringing accent of truth; but your scientific actor knows how he did it. He can repeat it again and again and again. He can be depended on. Once he has thought out his role and found the means to express his thought, he can always remember the means. And just as a master pianist may play with a different fire on different nights, but always strikes the same keys, so the skilled actor can use himself as a finely keyed instrument and thereon strike what notes he will. With due allowance for the varying mood and interest, the hundredth performance is as good as the first; or, for obvious reasons, far better. Genius is the great unknown quantity. Technique supplies a constant for the problem.

Stay out of the theatrical world, out of its petty interests, its inbreeding tendencies, its stifling atmosphere, its corroding influence. Once you become "theatricalized," you are lost, my friend; you are lost. Dwell in this artificial world, and you will know only the externals of acting. Never once will you have a renewal of inspiration.

Go into the streets, into the slums, into the fashionable quarters. Go into the day courts and the night courts. Become acquainted with sorrow, with many kinds of sorrow. Learn of the wonderful heroism of the poor, of the incredible generosity of the very poor. Go into the modest homes, into the out-of-the-way corners, into the open country. Go where you can find something fresh to bring back to the stage. There should be, there must be, a window open somewhere, a current of new air ever blowing through the theater. If as author, producer, director, or actor you become theatricalized, you are lost. The chance to do the fine thing may pass your way, but it is, not for you. You cannot do it. You have been spoiled. You have spoiled yourself.

It is in the irony of things that the theater

should be the most dangerous place for the actor. But, then, after all, the world is the worst possible place, the most corrupting place for the human soul. And just as there is no escape from the world, which follows us into the very heart of the desert, so the actor cannot escape the theater. And the actor who is a dreamer need not. All of us can only strive to remain uncontaminated. In the world we must be unworldly; in the theater the actor must be untheatrical.

When a part comes to you, establish your own ideal for it, and, striving for that, let no man born of woman, let nothing under the heavens, come between it and you. Pay no attention to the other actors unless they be real actors! Unless it is a bitter matter of bread and butter, pay no attention, or as little attention as possible, to the director, unless he is a real director. The chances are that he is wrong. The overwhelming chances are that he is "theatricalized," doing more harm than good. Do not let yourself be disturbed by his funny little ideas. Do not be corrupted, then, by the director.

And above all you must ignore the audience's pleasure or response. If you don't, you are lost forever. Then are you doomed indeed. Audiences, my friend, are variable, now quick, now slow, now cold, now warm. Sometimes they are like lovely violins, a beneficent privilege. Then you may be happy, but you must not count on it. An actor who is guided by the caprices of those across the footlights is soon in chaos. The real actor must be able to give as true a performance before three frigid persons as before a house packed to the brim with good-will. That is his business. Otherwise he is a helpless cork tossing on the waves.

After all, a piece of acting is not only a thing of science, but a work of art, something to be perfected by the actor according to the ideal that is within him. The painter does not work with his public at his side, the author does not write with his reader peering over his shoulder. The critic who is within every great artist should be his only acknowledged audience.

"Unrest of spirit is a mark of life; one problem after another presents itself and in the solving of them we can find our greatest pleasure."

—Kal Menninger

~111~

Here's a key word for True Actors: "interest." The dictionary tell us that interest is the state of wanting to know or learn about something or someone; it is the quality of exciting curiosity or holding the attention; and it's a subject about which one is concerned or enthusiastic.

I have been very fortunate to get to know a few of the truly great artists. The one thing I find that they all have in common is that they are deeply "interested." In what? In the world around them, in the people they are with, in discovering more about life and the vast possibilities for human behavior in this life.

Meryl Streep said, "I'm curious about other people. That's the essence of my acting. I'm interested in what it would be like to be you."

I want you to zoom in on the world around you and the people in your life and make a conscious practice of exercising your interest. Ask questions, connect, deepen your attention on the other, discover things you had no idea about, be surprised and amazed, get interested! Please do not do this as an effortful duty, but seek the joy in being a fully living and breathing member of this human race.

> "Life is a pure flame, and we live by
> an invisible sun within us."
>
> —Sir Thomas Brown

Enjoy some words on acting from Daniel Day-Lewis:

Perhaps I'm particularly serious, because I'm not unaware of the potential absurdity of what I'm doing. The work itself takes care of that part of one that might step aside and say: Is this a seemly thing to be doing, to be spending one's life dressing in other people's clothes? But at the same time, there's the potential for a certain kind of nobility in the work. Because, after all, if you're not exploring human experience in one form or another, it seems that maybe there's something missing in one's life. I love to see work on a screen. I like it that the camera is so penetrating. As much as it is unmerciful, I like that about it. In the theater you might be tempted to represent, rather than to be. And that goes against really everything that I felt I was trying to do, and everything that my training was based on. It's a joyful thing. It's very hard to explain that, even to myself. It's a paradox. Given the chance to enter into areas of one's soul, of one's experience, that can be extremely unsettling; nonetheless, there's great joy in the exploration of that. For me, at any rate. We do it with impunity. We're not held to account for it. It's a game; it always remains a game.

"You cannot depend on your eyes when your imagination is out of focus."

—Mark Twain

Let's talk about "doings." I prefer to call them "doings" but you may like to call them "actions" or "objectives." (Six of one, half dozen of the other.) Once you have a clear sense of what the character is really after in any particular beat of the scene, the key, then, to constructing the "doing" is in how you choose to say it to yourself. The words you choose are very important. Yes, of course, active verbs are most useful, for two big reasons. First, they incite you to take action specifically, and second, they are pointed toward the other person. Consider the impact of words like, "to beseech," "to scold," "to caution," "to intimidate," "to advise," "to correct," "to condemn," "to praise." You can see clearly how these "doings" compel you to do something specific and to do it in relationship to someone else.

A doing or action must never be general, require an emotional result, or be pointed at yourself. Here are a few actions that would not be effective or useful: "to get excited," "to be jealous," "to be shy," "to be furious." Do you see how these kinds of actions would put your attention more on yourself and lead to a generic and general emotional quality? Yes, these kinds of actions are disaster.

One last thing. The actual words you choose for your "doing" must have meaning to you; they must do something to you personally. This is what will help you actually want to do it.

> You cannot dream yourself into a character: you must hammer and forge yourself into one."
>
> —Henry D. Thoreau

~114~

> O heavy burden!
>
> POLONIUS
> I hear him coming. Let's withd...
>
> *Enter Prince Hamlet*   *Exeu...*
>
> HAMLET
> To be, or not to be; that is the qu
> Whether 'tis nobler in the mind to
> The slings and arrows of outrageou
> Or to take arms against a sea of tro
> And, by opposing, end them. To die,
> No more, and by a sleep to sa...

We have been discussing "doings" or "actions," and these are only some of the many choices you will be required to make as you work on the role. Whatever choices you make, they must be justified by the script. I am saying that if any particular choice you make is not congruent with the needs of the text, you have no right to that choice.

It is pretty obvious that we are not going to see a "happy-go-lucky" Hamlet anytime soon; "happy-go-lucky" is nowhere to be found in the psychological or emotional landscape of that particular text. But within that text is a vast variety of colors to bring to the role as you invest your own humanity into the work at hand. Remember, the script is your bible, and all inspiration is to be found there. This is not a limitation—no, quite the opposite. When you learn the skills of reading the script as a True Actor, this knowledge will set you free.

"The best way to make your dreams
come true is to wake up."

—Paul Valéry

~115~

The Chassidim say:

"Act each moment as if the whole universe were in perfect balance between the forces of good and evil: and it is your next action that is the final straw that will sway the whole of creation to one side or the other."

They also say:

"Your whole life is a rehearsal for the moment you are in now."

"It is of little traits that the greatest human character is composed."

—William Winter

~116~

Every human being knows suffering. Along the path, striving toward this thing we call True Acting, there may be some very difficult times. For today, I want to share some words from Rainer Maria Rilke that I have found most encouraging. They come from Letters to a Young Poet. I hope they will speak to you, as well:

> How could we forget those ancient myths that stand at the beginning of all races—the myths about dragons that at the last moment are transformed into princesses. Perhaps all the dragons in our lives are only princesses waiting for us to act, just once, with beauty and courage. Perhaps

everything that frightens us is, in its deepest essence, something helpless that wants our love.

So you must not be frightened if a sadness rises before you larger than any you've ever seen, if an anxiety like light and cloud shadows moves over your hands and everything you do. You must realize that something has happened to you; that life has not forgotten you; it holds you in its hands and will not let you fall. Why do you want to shut out of your life any uneasiness, any miseries, or any depressions? For after all, you do not know what work these conditions are doing inside you.

"The significance of a man is not in what he attains but in what he longs to attain."

—Khalil Gibran

~117~

I want to add to my previous tip, as I believe it is useful to have inspiration from others before us who have faced the dragons. Of course, these quotes also speak to the basic makeup of the great characters from dramatic literature, and I share them with you in this light.

From Abigail Adams:

"It is not in the still calm of life, or the repose of a pacific station, that great characters are formed. The habits of a vigorous mind are formed in contending with difficulties. All history will convince you of this, and that wisdom and penetration are the fruit of experience, not the lessons of retirement and leisure. Great necessities call out great virtues."

From Henri Frédéric Amiel:

"Conquering any difficulty always gives one a secret joy, for it means pushing back a boundary-line and adding to one's liberty."

From Johann Sebastian Bach:

"Every problem has a gift for you in its hands."

From Isak Dinesen:

"Difficult times have helped me to understand better than before, how infinitely rich and beautiful life is in every way, and that so many things that one goes worrying about are of no importance whatsoever."

From William Faulkner:

"People need trouble—a little frustration to sharpen the spirit on, toughen it. Artists do; I don't mean you need to live in a rat hole or gutter, but you have to learn fortitude, endurance."

From Harry Emerson Fosdick:

"He who knows no hardships will know no hardihood. He who faces no calamity will need no courage. Mysterious though it is, the characteristics in human nature which we love best grow in a soil with a strong mixture of troubles."

From Emmet Fox:

"It is the Law that any difficulties that can come to you at any time, no matter what they are, must be exactly what you need most at the moment, to enable you to take the next step forward by overcoming them. The only real misfortune, the only real tragedy, comes when we suffer without learning the lesson."

From Khalil Gibran:

"Pain and foolishness lead to great bliss and complete knowledge, for Eternal Wisdom created nothing under the sun in vain."

From Sydney Harris:

"When I hear somebody sigh, 'Life is hard,' I am always tempted to ask, 'Compared to what?'"

From Henry Miller:

"In this age, which believes that there is a short cut to everything, the greatest lesson to be learned is that the most difficult way is, in the long run, the easiest."

"Some men give up their designs when they have almost reached the goal; while others, on the contrary, obtain a victory by exerting, at the last moment, more vigorous efforts than before."

—Polybius

~118~

The only way to communicate to the audience in a way that reaches them "where they live" is through the actor's authentic experience in the moment. This authentic experience between two human beings onstage, along with the deep personal meaning that the True Actor has planted into his or her performance, induces a powerful personal response in the audience members that is out of their control and which they cannot anticipate.

This acting truth is generally thought to have appeared first with the work of Stanislavsky. But I want you to read a comment from the famous Japanese actor and playwright Zeami Motokiyo, who was the founder of Noh theater in the fifteenth century. Here Zeami describes the very same acting truth in a most simple and beautiful way:

"If, because the actor has noticed that old men walk with bent knees and back and have shrunken frames, he simply imitates these characteristics, he may achieve an appearance of decrepitude, but it will be at the expense of the "flower." And, if the "flower" be lacking, there will be no beauty in the impersonation. The "flower" consists in forcing upon an audience an emotion which they do not expect."

"Our plans miscarry because they have no aim.
When a man does not know what harbor he is
making for, no wind is the right wind."

—Seneca

~119~

The French actor Jean Vilar said:

"The actor is not a machine. This is a truism that has to be shouted in people's ears. The actor is neither parrot nor robot."

The renowned British stage actress Dame Ellen Terry was being directed by the kind of director we call a "traffic cop," who gave her the following instructions:

"At the rise of the curtain you are seen knitting at the table. After a count of fifteen, you rise, go to the window and look out. You then light a lamp on the mantelpiece. After that, you return to your seat at the table and resume your knitting."

"Yes," the actress responded, "and in the meantime, I'll do all those things for which I am paid so much money."

"When one door of happiness closes, another opens, but often we look so long at the closed door that we do not see the one that has been opened for us."

—Helen Keller

You must remember that if you fake emotion, it immediately communicates as false. Please note, the audience comes without any preconceived expectations for emotional results. What the audience responds to, always, is the simple truth.

You are the artist, and of course, you have a vision of the places you are striving to reach in your creation onstage. But what do you do when a particular moment is not in the emotional landscape you had hoped for? Your best choice, and the only useful choice, is to fully accept and embrace exactly where you are at and fully do what you are doing.

Unfortunately, in these moments, out of fear, most actors will push and strain to get the emotion "cooking," but this is a dead-end road, because now your attention is on yourself and you are no longer in the play. You are in your head. You are in your head watching yourself and calibrating the quality of your performance. To watch actors do this is quite unpleasant.

Again, the only way to handle these situations effectively is to accept where you are at and turn yourself over to your partner. If you give up all control, trust the moment, put your attention 100 percent on your partner, and do what you need to do (your "doing"), there is a good likelihood that the emotion will end up taking you by storm. What a great surprise.

"Fortify yourself with contentment, for this is an impregnable fortress."

—Epictetus

~121~

Let's employ my previous tip as the springboard for this one. There is another way I see actors often resisting their inner state rather than embracing it. Here's an example:

I was directing John Patrick Shanley's Savage In Limbo. (If you haven't read it, please do so—it is one of the great plays.) We had a wonderful actress playing "Savage," a thirty-two-year-old woman who is still a virgin and who is deeply isolated, lonely, stuck, and hungry to find a new way of living. One day in rehearsals, in the midst of a very raw moment in the play for Savage, the actress stopped and said, "I'm sorry, Larry, this just isn't working; I am not working."

I said, "Okay, tell me about it."

She responded with tears in her eyes, "Well, I just feel like I am so totally lost and like what I am doing isn't going anywhere, and nothing I am doing here is adding up, damn it! I just feel so goddam' stuck!"

I said, "Yes! And that's exactly what Savage is going through at this very moment, isn't it?"

The actress replied, "Yes, but . . ."

I said, "No buts! Accept those feelings. They are totally appropriate. Of course you are feeling stuck and deeply frustrated and that nothing you are doing is adding up. That's the story of Savage's life! Now leave yourself alone and do the scene again."

Well, she did, and it was beautiful, and her performance in the play was breathtaking. And the point I am making today is that if you allow the critical mind to lead, you will invariably stop the flow of discovery, missing the opportunity to deepen your connection with the character. So often, the actor will resist trusting that what he or she is experiencing is right on the mark. I have seen this happen countless times and with actors in every part of the world.

Your job? To get out of the way! You must accept and embrace exactly what you are experiencing and be the immediate and complete expression of this wave of life, always in response to your partners, moment by moment by moment.

> "Be not afraid of growing slowly; be
> afraid only of standing still."
>
> —Chinese proverb

~122~

Once the play opens, for most of the day, keep thoughts about the play at a distance, but find a time of the day when you start to shift your awareness to the world of the play. For me, it's when I begin my trip to the theater. As you begin this shift, do not think about going to the theater to perform; rather, allow the circumstances of the play to wash over you as the rapidly approaching major event in your life! From this point forward, the pressure intensifies, as you know there is something urgent and necessary that you must accomplish tonight. See the whole world, all the people you pass by on the street and the physical land-scape, through the point of view of the character. Let this continue as you enter your dressing room and put on your costume. By the time you make your entrance, you will be fully immersed and ready to take action.

"Insist on yourself. Never imitate."

—Ralph Waldo Emerson

~123~

When you are in the run of a play, your physical and psychological output are enormous. This is why the day after, you must find ways to recharge the battery and to refuel yourself for the next performance. If you were to spend the entire day, every day, focused on the play, you might deplete yourself to the point of madness. This is why I suggest that until you begin your journey to the theater, you find the most effective ways to nourish your body and your mind.

Yes, there are many actors who encourage personal suffering as a way of instigating their creativity. Personally, I think it is more effective to be a healthy human being who also acts.

"We are either progressing or retrograding
all the while; there is no such thing as
remaining stationary in this life."

—James Freeman Clarke

~124~

As for caring for yourself during the run of a play, True Acting Tips readers sent me some of their methods. The responses included many votes for physical activity, including vigorous exercise in the morning, yoga and martial arts classes, swimming at the beach, bike rides, walking among the trees, and Zumba! Then there were the more introspective ideas, such as meditation, reading a good novel, writing poetry, listening to favorite music, and watching classic movies. The other major category of suggestions I received were nutritional, including not eating dairy or sugar, eating lots of pasta, upping the supplements, treating oneself to very special chocolates, and a simple meal plan of a big breakfast, then a light lunch, but only a very small meal two hours before the show followed by a bigger meal after the show.

Now, for the following tip, I have a question I want you to consider:

"When you are in a play, how would you act the quality of love?"

"The best rules to form a young man are: to talk little, to hear much, to reflect alone upon what has passed in company, to distrust one's own opinions, and value others that deserve it."

—Sir William Temple

~125~

In the previous tip, I posed a question for you, "When you are in a play, how would you act the quality of love?"

This was a bit of a trick question, because the truth is, you cannot act the quality of love. The concept "love" is too big, and any attempt to act it would have to be "general," meaning mushy, artificial, and indicated. As True Actors, you never act the "quality" of anything, as this road will always lead you to the cliché. Please remember that one of the most important words in the actor's vocabulary is "specificity"!

So what is the correct approach?

To highlight the ingredients I will explain in a moment, I want to share with you a response from Kevin, a True Acting Tips reader. Here's what Kevin told us:

"Recently, I had a scene with an actress. We played a husband-and-wife couple. The script was about the couple sharing how they met and the ups and downs of their relationship. One night the actress came to the show very emotionally upset. No one knew why she was so upset. She would march onstage, go through the motions, then crumble into a corner backstage. Finally, it was our scene. While moving through the scene, I kept my attention on her and the pain she was hoping to hide. This created such a powerful connection for both of us. The emotions and true desire to comfort and protect her ignited our scene. After we left the stage, she turned around hugged me and with tear-filled eyes said, "Thank you."

What happened to Kevin was that, because of the unexpected emotional state of the actress playing his wife, he became completely available to her and he was injected into what we would call "authentic doing." Kevin now had a true desire to "comfort her" and a deep need to "protect her." And that's exactly what he did. And as he did these things, the scene "ignited" and the audience could feel Kevin's true love for his partner onstage.

In acting terms, we would call "to comfort" and "to protect" Kevin's "doings." That's the very simple answer to today's question. You must always know "specifically" what it is you are doing, and then you must do it out of an authentic need. In this way, you have a true experience, and so does the audience. Thanks to Kevin for sharing this wonderful moment onstage.

"Kind words are the music of the world."

—F. W. Faber

~126~

Acting students often cripple themselves with the pressure to "get it right." Here are some wise words from Olympic skater Scott Hamilton:

"You've got to fall down a lot. You've got to make a lot of mistakes. And you've got to fight for your place in the world, whatever it is. And you've got to take a lot of knocks, and you've got to spill some blood in order to get there. And that's part of the process."

"Every man is a volume if you know how to read him."
—William Ellery Channing

~127~

When you have a moment in the play when someone is knocking on your door and you have to answer the door and be surprised when you see who it is, how do you handle this acting challenge? The truth is that you know who is at the door and you must not know. Of course, this is one of the great demands of acting, "You know and you must not know."

To handle the knock-at-the-door example, most actors would open the door and pretend to be surprised. In other words, these actors would try to "make it look like" they are surprised. This is called "indicating" or, as we have established previously, "trying to make it look like something is happening when nothing is happening." This way of handling the moment will be communicated as false. As a True Actor, you know that you must have an authentic experience of being surprised when you answer the door rather than pretend to be surprised.

This tip is something I know you are going to love, because it so simple and so much fun to work with. It is called "Expectancy." Here's how it works . . .

Again, you are in the play and there will be a knock on the door, and you must not know who it is, and you need to be surprised when you answer the door. Simply make a choice as to who you are "expecting" to arrive at your door. The choice must be specific and in alignment with the world of the play.

It might be that you are expecting the dry cleaners to deliver some clothes you need for an important meeting, or the cable guy is going to repair the Internet so you can get online and check for an important email. The choice is personal to you, meaning, you make it up and then use it in your rehearsals until the meaning of the knock on the door becomes habitual. After some practice, you will hear the knock and automatically, your inner response will be, "Oh, good, the cable guy is here, I can check for that email!" Then, when you open the door to greet the cable guy, you will actually be surprised to see the other character in the play who is waiting to come in. See how this works? Now the audience will believe that you are surprised, because you are! Beautiful.

"Go back a little to leap further."

—John Clarke

~128~

When you work on a role, find every place you can, especially when you have any kind of physical activity onstage, to make things more difficult on yourself rather than easier. This is exactly the opposite of the way many actors work. Many actors want it to be easy. I am telling you to look for all opportunities to make things more challenging, and in the smallest details.

For example, let's say that in one moment onstage you have to open a book to a specific page so that you can read a poem to your scene partner. Many actors would have that page clearly bookmarked so that they could turn to it easily and read the poem. I suggest that you make it hard to find that page. Bookmark the wrong page so that you must search to find the correct one. You might even have the stage manager put the bookmark in a different place every night so that you never know where it will be and you will always encounter a new problem when you open the book. Hey, put some gum between the pages that have the poem so that you have to separate the pages carefully and not rip the poem, which would make it impossible to read!

Finding the poem is a very simple example of understanding a "way of working" with yourself. I want you to get to the place where you welcome surprises and where you set up your world onstage so that everything is more pressing and difficult for you. Why do you think I would ask you to do this? It is only when things are more difficult that greater demands are placed on you, taking you into the "unknown," which is the one and only place true creation is possible. Also, your involvement in accomplishing these kinds of demanding activities bring a tremendous sense of reality to your work that communicates to the audience, "This is actually happening." And, by the way, it's fun.

> "Half of the failures in life come from
> pulling one's horse when he is leaping."
>
> —Thomas Hood

~129~

I want to highlight the fact that acting is not about the words; True Acting is much, much more about what makes the words necessary. Due to the urgency of this message, I want to add to the conversation with some beautiful words from Peter Brook:

> A word does not start as a word—it is an end product which begins as an impulse, stimulated by attitude and behavior which dictate the need for expression. This process occurs inside the dramatist; it is repeated inside the actor. Both may only be conscious of the words, but both for the author and then for the actor the word is a small

visible portion of a gigantic unseen formation. Some writers attempt to nail down their meaning and intentions in stage directions and explanations, yet we cannot help being struck by the fact that the best dramatists explain themselves the least. They recognize that the only way to find the true path to the speaking of a word is through a process that parallels the original creative one. This can neither be by-passed nor simplified.

Don't you love that image, a "gigantic unseen formation?" Yes, that is our job! When we deal with this gigantic unseen formation, we will discover the "true path to the speaking of a word." Without it, the words are hollow and without life and will leave the audience cold.

"It is not work that kills men, it is worry. Work is healthy; you can hardly put more on a man than he can bear. But worry is rust upon the blade. It is not movement that destroys the machinery, but friction."

—Henry Ward Beecher

~130~

With True Acting, as in life itself, the most important things are those that are unseen. The word "unseen" is a key word in our craft, for it is the life the actor has planted inside the text that makes a performance captivating and deeply moving. Today, I offer you some illuminating words from theater critic and author Walter Kerr:

> A letter came to me a few years ago from a long-retired actress who had, as a youngster, been taken to see Edwin Booth play King Lear. It seems that towards the end of the play, when the mad Lear was brought face to face with his daughter Cordelia, there was a sharp pause,

then—for a second that couldn't quite be caught or measured—a startled, desperate, longing flicker of near-recognition stirred somewhere behind the old man's eyes, and then—nothing. The entire audience rose, without thinking, to its feet. It didn't cheer. It simply stood up. It was as though a single electrical discharge had passed from one body on the stage, instantaneously, through a thousand bodies in the auditorium. Something had been plugged into a socket; two forces had met. This meeting is what the theater is all about; it is its greatest power. The theater gains its natural—and unique—effect not from the mere presence of live actors, or the happy accident of an occasional lively audience, but from existence of a live relationship between these two indispensable conspirators, signaling to one another through space.

"I never think of the future—it comes soon enough."
—Albert Einstein

~131~

One of my favorite playwrights is John Patrick Shanley. I have been fortunate to both act in and direct some of his plays. Consider his description of the ground we must walk on as we travel the path toward True Acting and some of the demons we encounter on this journey:

> A man in our society is not left alone. Not in the cities. Not in the woods. We must have commerce with our fellows, and that commerce is difficult and uneasy. I do not understand how to live in society. I don't get it. Each person has an enormous effect. Call it environmental impact if you like. Where my foot falls, I leave a mark, whether I want

to or not. We are linked together, each to each. You can't breathe without taking a breath from somebody else. You can't smile without changing the landscape. And so I ask the question: Why is theatre so ineffectual, unnew, not exciting, fussy, not connected to the thrilling recognition possible is dreams?

It is a question of spirit. My ungainly spirit thrashes around inside me, making me feel lumpy and sick. My spirit is this moment dissatisfied with the outward life I inhabit. Why does my outward life not reflect the enormity of the miracle of existence? Why are my eyes blinded with always new scales, my ears stopped with thick chunks of fresh wax, why are my fingers calloused again? I don't ask these questions lightly. I beat on the stone door of my tomb. I want out! Some days I wake up in a tomb, some days on a grassy mound by a river. Today I woke up in a tomb. Why does my spirit sometimes retreat into a deathly closet? Perhaps it is not my spirit leading the way at such times, but my body, longing to lie down in marble gloom and rot away.

Theatre is a safe place to do the unsafe things that need to be done. When it's not a safe place, it's abusive to actors and to audiences alike. When its safety is used to protect cowards masquerading as heroes, it's a boring travesty. An actor who is truly heroic reveals the divine that passes through him, that aspect of himself that he does not own and cannot control. The control and the artistry of the heroic actor is in service to his soul.

We live in an era of enormous cynicism. Do not be fooled.

Don't act for money. You'll start to feel dead and bitter.

Don't act for glory. You'll start to feel dead, fat and fearful.

We live in an era of enormous cynicism. Do not be fooled.

Act from the depth of your feeling imagination. Act for celebration, for search, for grieving, for worship, to express that desolate sensation of wandering through the howling wilderness. Don't worry about Art. Do these things and it will be Art.

"If you kick a stone in anger, you'll hurt your own foot."
—Korean proverb

"Not the fastest horse can catch a word spoken in anger."
—Chinese proverb

"Anger is a bad counselor."
—French proverb

~132~

Many times in my life, I have been led to people who would become my most important "teachers." I don't mean teachers in the literal sense, as in being enrolled in a school and going to class, but certainly, in the classroom of my life, these individuals opened up doors for me, offered lessons in being fully human, and uncovered paths toward healing that carried me to places I never dreamed were possible.

You and I have been defining a very specific quest. And, though this particular journey is certainly not for everyone, by giving you a continually clearer picture of what this thing called True Acting really is, my intention has continually been to offer you the opportunity to see if these values mesh with your own deepest desire.

I have talked a number of times about the huge challenges that come to all of us who are striving toward True Acting and have said that, along with these challenges, we will often experience tremendous suffering. My own belief is that suffering is built into the equation and that only through the commitment to continue, even when the pain and the fear threaten to swallow us whole, do we discover that joy is waiting on the other side. This has certainly been my experience time and time again. I offer you this quote from Emmet Fox:

"It is the Law that any difficulties that can come to you at any time, no matter what they are, must be exactly what you need most at the moment, to enable you to take the next step forward by overcoming them. The only real misfortune, the only real tragedy, comes when we suffer without learning the lesson."

I wanted to discuss this with you because the truth is, when barriers to your work come up in class, places where you experience real "stuckness," there will not always be the means to address these issues in the classroom. Yes, your acting teachers must help you in every way possible, to the best of their ability, in relationship to you the human being and your process of learning the craft of acting. But sometimes, the difficulties you encounter will not be appropriate to address in the classroom, as an acting class must never veer into the realm of therapy session. The acting class that is a therapy session in disguise is both dangerous and harmful and must be avoided at all costs.

This means that you, the artist, must search out other means to move beyond anything that is holding you back from being completely expressive and fully present and available. And this is where you will meet your other important teachers.

As a very young college student, while spending the summer as part of a theater troupe that performed original plays in the outdoor theater at a resort craft village in the Catskill Mountains of New York, I would walk past a stained-glass shop every day on the way to the performance. I would always stop to look at the beautiful stained-glass artwork hanging in its window, and one day when I had time off from rehearsals and performances, I went in to meet the artist. Her name was Beverly, and when I talked on and on about how her stained-glass pieces had excited and moved me, she simply asked, "Would you like to learn how to do it?"

That day, I became Beverly's apprentice, and for the rest of the summer, whenever I had time, I was standing by her side at the big wood table, learning how to cut glass and work with foil and solder to make stained-glass boxes.

As I worked with Beverly, I not only received the lessons of making stained glass, but I had my first exposure to a person who was mindful, present, and deeply available. It was earthshaking for me. Beverly never talked about anything personal with me, and I never asked. In silence mostly, we concentrated on the glass making, with Beverly gently prompting me to make minor adjustments as I worked with these new tools. But one day, I overheard her talking about spiritual matters and about meditation groups with a friend who had come to visit from Brooklyn, and Beverly sensed my interest. The next day, Beverly handed me a few sheets of paper and said, "Here, read this, you may enjoy it."

Well, the "lecture" she gave me to read was written as if the person knew all the pain I had in my heart and the ways I could begin to heal those childhood hurts. This was the beginning of my becoming a member of a community called the "Pathwork." I mention this because I attribute some of my success in my classes with Sandy Meisner at the playhouse, and my growth there as a young actor, to the work I was doing in the Pathwork group. Each week, as new challenges and difficulties came up in my acting classes, I had this wonderful place to go and explore it all and then return with a greater strength to leap into the acting work.

If you would like to know more about the Pathwork, you may visit them on the web at www.pathwork.org.

Here is someone else I want you to know about. Her name is Tara Brach, and she is a western teacher of Buddhist meditation, emotional healing, and spiritual awakening. First, she is one of those rare, completely loving souls with a gentle directness that speaks right into the heart. Also, the work she does and which she offers so generously—on her website, in her books and CDs, and in video podcasts—is completely related to the art of True Acting and the depth of humanity it requires.

If you have the desire to take your work deeper and are looking for a beautiful voice in this world to assist you on your way, please visit www.tarabrach.com. Also, you will find an interview with Tara, and an introduction to meditation from her, in the resource chapter of this book.

"We have no right to ask when sorrow comes, "Why did this happen to me?" unless we ask the same question for every moment of happiness that comes our way."

—Author unknown

~133~

A fable for you:

The Wise Woman's Stone

A wise woman who was traveling in the mountains found a precious stone in a stream. The next day she met another traveler, who was hungry, and the wise woman opened her bag to share her food. The hungry traveler saw the precious stone and asked the woman to give it to him. She did so without hesitation.

The traveler left, rejoicing in his good fortune. He knew the stone was worth enough to give him security for a lifetime.

But a few days later he came back to return the stone to the wise woman.

"I've been thinking," he said. "I know how valuable the stone is, but I give it back in the hope that you can give me something even more precious. Give me what you have within you that enabled you to give me the stone.

"If I had a formula for bypassing trouble, I would not pass it round. Trouble creates a capacity to handle it. I don't embrace trouble; that's as bad as treating it as an enemy. But I do say meet it as a friend, for you'll see a lot of it and had better be on speaking terms with it."

—Oliver Wendell Holmes

~134~

All jobs have one thing in common: they were brought into existence because they are supposed to make a difference in someone else's life.

Acting is a job.

When you bolster yourself to work in the space I call True Acting, you actually do make a difference in the lives of the people who witness you. As David Mamet said:

"People come to the theatre to be reminded that authentic communication between two human beings is still possible!"

When you work simply and honestly and with meaning, you are not just making a wonderful production for people to come experience and enjoy—you are, in fact, the gift.

"I ask not for a lighter burden, but for broader shoulders."

—Jewish proverb

"Bad is never good until worse happens."

—Danish proverb

"Smooth seas do not make skillful sailors."

—African proverb

"If the thunder is not loud, the peasant
forgets to cross himself."

—Russian proverb

~135~

My advice, if you want to be a better actor, is to first be a better person.

As I have been teaching around this country, and many other countries, this is a value that has become a primary concern for actors and teachers. I am thrilled with the movement in this direction, because the act of creating theater must be rooted first in human values or it is false.

It is not that theater is an imitation of our lives; it's not. Theater, as Sandy Meisner told us, demands a greater truth. What is this greater truth? It is a basic life truth; the things we know in our hearts that have lasting value always come to us as a gift through our connection with someone else. The best things in life, from my point of view (and certainly this has been my experience time and time again), are surprising, unexpected, and greater than we could have imagined, and they are always the result of being in relationship with others.

When we seriously consider the path toward true satisfaction and fulfillment in this life, we can see that this path always travels through someone else. It is the same with acting. Acting does not fuel our acting, and it never has. Without our humanity as the key, the impulse to act will fade, because it is shallow, limited, and just not much fun.

I love the way William Ernest Hocking expressed it: "We cannot climb up a rope that is attached only to our own belt."

"If you woke up breathing, congratulations!
You have another chance."

—Andrea Boydston

~136~

Training as Invitation

I have witnessed and experienced a deep aching in actors and acting teachers in every part of the world. Much of the acting community and the teaching community have become deeply weary of the arguments over technique and frustrated by the cold and lifeless results of various teaching methods in the classroom.

On the flip side of the coin, I have also witnessed the great enjoyment some theater instructors get out of arguing about technique and attempting to convince others that their particular system is the best. I have always found these arguments fruitless and boring. Also, it is interesting that many of the most severe attacks have come from people who have never actually practiced or personally explored the techniques they are condemning. I have experienced this kind of teacher as a person who comes from the attitude that if his neighbor breaks his leg, it will make him, the teacher, walk better. I find this incredibly sad, and, of course, this way of approaching life goes against everything our art is about.

Here is a quote from Herbert Spencer that speaks eloquently about this matter:

"There is a principle which is a bar against all information, which is proof against all arguments and which cannot fail to keep a man in everlasting ignorance. That principle is contempt prior to investigation."

As a teacher, I am not here to convince anyone of anything. I think of my work with students, always, as an invitation. The truth about technique, to me, is that if it helps you, great, and if it doesn't, throw it away. Of course, I do have a particular passion for training an actor, and my whole adult life has been a devotion to the Meisner approach, but it is a leaning that comes not from any concept, but from my direct experience of a particular path that I was rigorously trained in, which saved my life as an actor and as a human being and which made absolute sense to my insides.

For me, just as I train my students to earn the right to speak the playwright's words, I believe I can make a difference in the lives of my students and help them to grow only when I teach from a place of true knowing; knowing not as theory but as a living, breathing part of my being.

"We too should make ourselves empty, that the great soul of the universe may fill us with its breath."

—Laurence Binyon

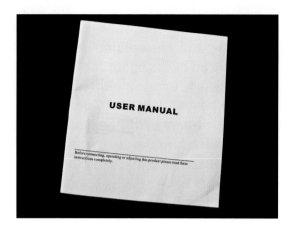

The foundation exercise in the Meisner technique is called "repetition." Over the years, I found that many people are not really clear on the ultimate purpose of repetition. One thing is for sure, repetition is not about "reading" behavior. I have often heard this interpretation forwarded, and it is misleading because it suggests that repetition is something technical, like getting good at reading the instructions to build an Ikea bookshelf. This is not repetition.

I remember, when I was a very young acting student, seeing the great Norwegian actress Liv Ullmann in an interview with Dick Cavett. He asked her how she makes being in love in front of a camera so real when it is called for in a scene with another actor. She told him that it simply has to do with "opening herself" to the other actor.

Cavett asked her if she could show him what she was talking about, and she agreed. Then, without a word, she did exactly what she said. She opened herself to him. In that moment, I experienced her as being deeply in love with Dick Cavett, and I suddenly found myself sitting on my couch weeping, it was so beautiful, both the overwhelming power of her love and the mastery of this art I was striving to learn.

What I want you to know is that, in those moments of deep connection, when not a word was spoken, Liv Ullmann was, in fact, doing repetition!

The practice of repetition must lead toward the ability to be in communion with another human being; it is a sharing at the most intimate, human level. Although the process begins with words, repetition has nothing at all to do with speaking. Repetition is continually aimed at reawakening the natural and organic human ability for people to be involved with each other, for it is this involvement that then makes words, silence, and all of human behavior necessary.

Like all art, repetition and the Meisner approach in all of its meticulous, step-by-step components, lifts the actor to the spiritual experience where the actor actually becomes an empty vessel, and where something greater than the actor can express itself through him. Through the work, the actor's attention becomes directed completely outward and connected to the world around him, with no need to control or manipulate anyone as he fights with his life to achieve the mission he has set out on, the mission that was inspired by the script and has now become truly his own.

"Nobody grows old merely by living a number of years. We grow old by deserting our ideals. Years may wrinkle the skin, but to give up enthusiasm wrinkles the soul."

—Samuel Ullman

~138~

True Acting comes from a deep state of "knowing," knowing what we are doing and knowing what we are talking about; "knowing" not as an intellectual concept but rather, as a living reality.

Here is an often-related story about Gandhi:

For many hours, a woman and her eight-year-old son were waiting in the long line to talk with Gandhi. Finally, it was her turn to approach Gandhi and ask her question. "Gandhi, my son is causing great trouble in school and they are threatening to throw him out. The doctor told me that his bad behavior is caused by eating too much sugar." Gandhi looked at the boy and then told the mother, "Bring the boy back to me in two weeks."

Two weeks later, the woman and her son found themselves in another very long line. After many hours, she approached Gandhi once again. "Gandhi, two weeks ago, I told you that my son was going to be thrown out of school if he did not behave and that his behavior was caused by him eating too much sugar." Gandhi looked down at the boy and said, "Stop eating sugar."

As the woman and the boy began to walk away, the mother stopped and turned back to Gandhi. "Gandhi, why did you make us come back today and wait for many hours to speak with you? Why didn't you tell my son to stop eating sugar two weeks ago?" Gandhi replied, "Because until two weeks ago, I, too, was eating sugar."

"If your work speaks for itself, don't interrupt."
—Henry J. Kaiser

~139~

We recognize that on the path toward True Acting, we will face many challenges. Some will come along when least expected and may feel too overpowering to survive.

Enjoy the parable of the mule:

> Once there was a farmer who owned an old mule. One day the mule fell into the farmer's well and the farmer heard the mule braying, or whatever mules do when they fall into wells.
>
> After carefully assessing the situation, the farmer sympathized with the mule but decided that neither the mule nor the well was worth the trouble of saving.
>
> Instead, he called his neighbors together, told them what had happened, and enlisted them to

help haul dirt to bury the old mule in the well and put him out of his misery.

Initially, the old mule was hysterical. But as the farmer and his neighbors continued shoveling and the dirt hit his back, a thought struck him. It dawned on him that every time a shovel load of dirt landed on his back, he could shake it off and step up! This he did, blow after blow. Shake it off and step up, shake it off and step up, shake it off and step up.

He repeated this to encourage himself. No matter how painful the blows, or how distressing the situation seemed, the old mule fought panic and just kept right on shaking it off and stepping up.

It wasn't long before the old mule, battered and exhausted, stepped triumphantly over the wall of that well. What seemed like it would bury him actually helped him, all because of the manner in which he handled his adversity.

That's life. If we face our problems and refuse to give in to panic, bitterness, or self-pity, the adversities that come along to bury us usually have within them the very real potential to benefit us.

> "Creativity is allowing yourself to make mistakes. Art is knowing which ones to keep."
>
> —Scott Adams

~140~

Here's a little story I find thrilling every time I read it. It comes from Arthur Miller's autobiograhy Timebends. Here, Miller speaks about Lee Cobb preparing to open in the original production of Death of a Salesman, directed by Elia Kazan:

> As rehearsals proceeded, Lee seemed to move about in a buffalo's stupefied trance, muttering his lines, plodding with deathly slowness from posi-tion to position, and behaving like a man who had been punched in the head. "He's just learning it," Kazan shakily reassured me after three or four days. I waited as a week went by, and then ten days, and all that was emerging from Lee Cobb's

throat was a bumpy hum.

On about the twelfth day, in the afternoon, Lee stood up as usual from the bedroom chair and turned to Mildred Dunnock and bawled, "No, there's more people now . . . There's more people!" and, gesturing toward the empty upstage where the window was supposed to be, caused a block of apartment houses to spring up in my brain, and the air became sour with the smell of kitchens where once there had been only the odors of earth, and he began to move frighteningly, with such ominous reality that my chest felt pressed down by an immense weight. After the scene had gone on for a few minutes, I glanced around to see if the others had my reaction. Jim Proctor had his head bent into his hands and was weeping. Eddie Kook was looking shocked, almost appalled, and tears were pouring over his cheeks, and Kazan behind me was grinning like a fiend, gripping his temples with both hands, and we knew we had it—there was an unmistakable wave of life moving across the air of the empty theater, a wave of Willy's pain and protest.

I began to weep myself at some point that was not particularly sad, but was as much, I think, out of pride in our art, in Lee's magical capacity to imagine, to collect within himself every mote of life since Genesis and to let it pour forth. He stood up there like a giant moving the Rocky Mountains into position.

By the way, if you have not read Timebends, you really must; it is one of the great books for the True Actor in training.

"The aim of every artist is to arrest motion, which is life, by artificial means and hold it fixed so that a hundred years later, when a stranger looks at it, it moves again since it is life."

—William Faulkner

~141~

Recently a friend of mine, a wonderful actress and member of Actors' Equity, told me that she was asked by the artistic director of a theater to change her name so that he could hire her as a non-equity performer. Disgusted and disappointed in the director, she turned down the offer without blinking an eye. Listen, if a union theater wants to cast you in a show, and you are a member of Actors' Equity, they should go to their donors and raise the money to hire you under an Equity contract! There is a tremendous lack of integrity in asking a union actress to work under a false name and jeopardize her union membership. It is just not the right thing to do! As John Proctor says in The Crucible:

> "Because it is my name! Because I cannot have another in my life! Because I lie and sign myself to lies! Because I am not worth the dust on the feet of them that hang! How may I live without my name? I have given you my soul; leave me my name!"

I thought it would be useful today, for all of you who are either members of Actors' Equity now or hoping to become members, to give you some words on the matter directly from the Actors' Equity Union. Especially because, when you live in any of the smaller markets, there will always be more non-union work available than roles that will come with an Equity contract.

Here's what Actors' Equity says:

> "When is it okay for me to work without an Equity contract?" The best (and shortest) answer is "never." There is never a reason for an Equity member to work without a contract. Accepting such work undermines the union's considerable efforts to maintain standards for professional actors and stage managers. Often, by involving Equity, terms can be reached with even the most reluctant producers to bring the show under contract.
>
> "But this theatre is really small-time . . . But this gig is really short . . . But I'm just doing it as

a favor . . ." Equity has endeavored to be flexible by creating contracts that cover all levels of work. Agreements such as Special Appearance, Guest Artist, Business Theatre, and Staged Reading can often be utilized to bring the work onto Equity contract. If you're wondering, call Equity!

"I live in a "right-to-work" state. Doesn't that mean I have the right to work without an Equity Contract?" No. It does not. "Right-to-work" does not impact upon your obligations as an Equity member. Once you have joined, you have agreed never to work without an Equity contract.

"What could happen if I am discovered working without benefit of contract?" First of all, there is the moral penalty of knowing you have betrayed your fellow union members. But there are steep tangible liabilities, as well. In accordance with Equity's Constitution and By-Laws, a Charges Hearing Committee is convened. It hears the case and decides on the remedy. Penalties can include fines, letters of apology to the membership, and even expulsion from the union.

"Can I resign to work non-Equity, then rejoin?" Equity membership is a hard-won honor and something of which to be proud. Many actors dream of the day they "get their card." It is not a commodity to be traded for financial gain or convenience. Unfortunately, some actors do make the choice to leave Equity to take non-union work. Often, those actors wish to rejoin the union later. In that event, their case must go before the President's Planning Committee. Sometimes the actor is allowed to rejoin (after paying any fines and/or fees—including initiation—that may be exacted), and sometimes not.

"What if my agent sends me for non-Equity work?" Equity's agency regulations state that an agent who knowingly advises a member to seek non-union employment is subject to a fine of $5,000 for a first offense and additional penalties, including loss of franchise for subsequent offenses.

Finally, today's professional performers must be able to work in every medium: theatre, television, radio, film, the internet and other new media platforms. To protect the wages and working conditions that everyone deserves, members of one union must not undermine another union's efforts to organize professional work opportunities.

"When my daughter was about seven years old, she asked me one day what I did at work. I told her I worked at the college, that my job was to teach people how to draw. She stared at me, incredulous, and said, "You mean they forget?"

—Howard Ikemoto

~142~

I have talked about choosing a way of saying your "doings" or "actions" that have personal meaning to you so that it will incite you to take action. Of course, this is true with every choice you make; they all need to be deeply appetizing to you, and what this means, always, is intimate and specific to you.

I think Jack Nicholson expressed this quite beautifully when he said:

"Most actors' problems, professional or amateur, deal with tension and there are a lot of devices and ways of eliminating it. In a very professional actor the tension is because they haven't made a choice that has taken enough of their mental interest. In other words, they haven't made a vital enough choice; it's not up to a level that will engage their imagination and get them into pretending un-self-consciously."

"If you don't get everything you want, think of the things you don't get that you don't want."

—Oscar Wilde

~143~

Whatever acting approaches you happen to study as an actor in training, ultimately you must develop your own, very personal technique of acting. From all the good and useful things you learn, from those methods that best fit your most intimate inner mechanics, you will establish a distinctive way of working. And what you call this way of working is totally irrelevant.

I love these words from director Peter Brook:

> Outstanding actors, like all real artists, have
> some mysterious psychic chemistry, half conscious

and yet three quarters hidden, that they themselves may only define as "instinct," "hunch," "my voices," that enables them to develop their vision and their art. Special cases may follow special rules: one of the greatest actresses of our time who seems in rehearsals to be observing no method whatsoever actually has an extraordinary system of her own which she can only articulate in nursery language. "Kneading the flour today, darling," she has said to me. "Putting it back to bake a bit longer"; "Need some yeast now"; "We're basting this morning." No matter: this is precise science, just as much as if she gave it the terminology of the Actors' Studio.

"He who has so little knowledge of human nature as to seek happiness by changing anything but his own disposition will waste his life in fruitless efforts."

—Samuel Johnson

~144~

Relevant quote for the True Actor in training from Frederick Buechner:

"You can kiss your family goodbye and put miles between you, but at the same time, you carry then with you in your heart, your mind, your stomach, because you do not just live in a world but a world lives in you."

"Optimist: someone who isn't sure whether life is a tragedy or a comedy but is tickled silly just to be in the play."

—Robert Brault

~145~

When we talk about "character," what we are really refer-ring to is a specific point of view, how the person views the world. Mostly, we have talked about approaching character from the psychological. We call this working from the "in-side-out." Of course, there is another path to authentically inhabit the point of view of the character, and this is using a physical condition, which we call working from the "outside-in." This approach is just as valid and must arrive at the same human truths.

I want you to try a very simple exercise and see how a physical condition can start to impact the way you see the world. Take a half hour when you are in a public place that is busy and where you can walk around and engage with people. A supermarket or a department store or a shopping mall are some good ideas. Then, I want you to move at a pace that is faster than you normally move. Do everything faster. Walk faster, look at items you might buy more quickly, talk with people in the store more rapidly, and then briskly move on to someone else. Keep going in this swift manner for half an hour, but not because you are in a hurry to get anywhere; simply adopt this physical life as if it is your normal way of operating in the world. How does it feel to be a person who goes through life this way? What does it do to you emotionally to encounter other people from this perspective?

In the very popular television series *All in the Family*, which ran from 1971 to 1979, the brilliant actress Jean Stapleton did this very thing. She played the character Edith Bunker, called the "Dingbat" by her husband, Archie. If you can get a hold of some of the episodes, you will see that Edith never walked, she always ran. It didn't matter where she was going in the house or what she was doing, she always ran to do it—taking care of the family, serving food to Archie, sorting the laundry. It was a beautiful choice, and it affected every aspect of her being.

"Since the house is on fire let us warm ourselves."

—Italian proverb

"Turn your face to the sun and the
shadows fall behind you."

—Maori proverb

"Those who wish to sing, always find a song."

—Swedish proverb

~146~

In the previous tip, I asked you to do activities such as walking and speaking more rapidly than normal for you. I asked how it feels to be a person who goes through life this way—what does it do to you emotionally to encounter other people from this perspective?

I want to share a wonderful response to the exercise from True Acting Tips reader Carol in Seattle:

> Hi, Larry, I am a senior actress out here in Seattle and I thought, what a fun assignment; I had never tried anything like it. Also, having a longtime meditation practice, I always try to slow things down in life so I can remain mindful of my surroundings. I thought, what a great challenge!

So, I went over to the Pike Place Market, and as I approached the fish vendors, I began to walk faster and I kept up this rapid pace for about forty minutes. I went from stall to stall, talking fast with the people selling cheese, coffee, antiques, candles, and rugs. I ran around shopping for roasted cashews, used books, chocolates, fruits, and spices, all the while looking quickly at everything and trying to make a fast decision whether I wanted to buy it or not. I did not give anyone much of my time, because I had to get going to someone and something else!

Wow, this really was powerful. I felt emotionally hungry, like I wanted the world to give me more, that there wasn't enough to fill me up and I had to have more. I also started to feel like I was only interested in what people could give to me or do for me, and if they didn't do it right away, well, I had enough of them. I also really felt a strong sense of not wanting people to really see me and that it was none of their business anyway. Whew, by the end of the forty minutes, I really hooked into a very scary closeness to being this kind of deeply needy person, and it shook me up! Thanks so much for this physical exercise; what a wonderful new way to approach connecting with a character's way of thinking, feeling, and behaving!

Thank you Carol. Carol really gets to the heart of what this kind of physical experiment can lead to and how useful it can be when exploring the character's point of view, opening new doors that you may never have expected.

Now a new assignment: let's try the reverse condition with a small addition. Here's your mission, should you choose to accept it:

This time, again in a busy public location, I want you to move more slowly and carefully then you normally move, and do everything at a slower pace. Now, in addition to moving slowly, I want you to take on a new posture. Walk with your belly pushed out and your shoulders and head pulled back. Think of this as walking with your belly leading the way and your head following along from the rear. Don't make this posture too extreme; think of it as a very subtle shift of the eyes looking over the belly which is leading you around in life. Give this a try.

> "At bottom every man knows well enough that he is a unique being, only once on this earth; and by no extraordinary chance will such a marvelously picturesque piece of diversity in unity as he is, ever be put together a second time."
>
> —Friedrich Nietzsche

~147~

In the previous tip, the physical exercise I asked you to explore called for moving more slowly and carefully than normal in a busy public location, with your belly subtly pushed out. I share with you a response sent in by True Acting Tips reader Millie in São Paulo, Brazil:

> I went to visit a friend of mine who attends FAAP University. She was in class and I had about half an hour to just walk around campus while I waited to meet her for coffee. I did exactly what you asked us to do—I walked slowly and I took on this interesting posture. I am also a dancer, so I found it very intriguing to lead with my

stomach and have the feeling that my head was following from behind. As you said, I made this a subtle change, but the impact on me emotionally was huge. I suddenly felt that I was arrogant and owned the world and that all these common people I passed by had such meaningless lives compared with mine. One person actually came up to me and asked for directions to a building and out of my mouth came, "Excuse me, are you talking to me?"

The person responded to my unpleasant attitude with, "Yes, do you know?" and I said, "I don't have time for that." I didn't plan to say any of this, it just popped right out. The more I walked the campus in this way, the more I resented that my so-called friend was keeping me waiting this long, and I considered just leaving without telling her. Finally, she did come running up to me, and I had to really shake off the posture and the emotional attitude! I told her about my experience over coffee, and she was quite impressed. Thank you! This exercise was like a light bulb turning on for me, and I know it will be useful in both my acting and my dance!"

Thank you, Millie. There you go, working from the "outside-in." Another great option for you as you explore the character's point of view.

To review, when you work on the character's point of view from the "inside-out," it must lead you to authentic human behavior, and when you begin from physical behavior, as we did today, it must lead you to an authentic emotional and psychological point of view toward the world. Both approaches are wonderful and both totally viable.

"No man for any considerable period can wear one face to himself and another to the multitude, without finally getting bewildered as to which may be the true."

—Nathaniel Hawthorne

~148~

As we have established, a "particularization" is a technique of personalizing a specific moment in the script, a moment that occurs in the midst of a scene and that requires you to have a powerful emotional response. Obviously, you cannot stop the action of the play to prepare for this moment. Rather, you must make the strong, personal meaning of this moment "habitual" so that it occurs without you having to think about it.

A particularization is actually an "as-if." You must say to yourself, "This moment is 'as-if'—what is happening for me?" The moments in a play that will need to be worked on in this way usually occur when characters receive major, unexpected news or have something unanticipated happen to them.

Here's a fabulous twist on approaching a particularization . . .

In a play I acted in many years ago, I had to have a deep and strong emotional response to the opening of an envelope that the character always carried around in his pocket. The way I handled it was by personalizing what I expected to see when I opened the envelope. I made that item very meaningful to me. Then, when I actually opened the envelope to discover that it was, in fact, empty, it was a devastating blow!

So, the approach? Consider personalizing a moment by the absence of something being there. What I mean is, you first create the expectation that something important to you will be where it is supposed to be, and in the specific moment that you are particularizing, it is suddenly not there! If you look at Clifford Odets's Waiting for Lefty, this is exactly what the actor who is playing Joe has to do when he comes home to Edna and discovers that all of the furniture is missing from his home.

"Nobody is bored when he is trying to make something that is beautiful, or to discover something that is true."

—William Inge

~149~

I have seen many actors enter the audition room with an adversarial attitude that makes the event a very unpleasant experience for everyone involved.

The truth is, at the moment of the audition, the director or the casting director is the best friend you have. I am not saying you should adopt this attitude as a manipulative tactic; I say it because it happens to be true. They want you to be great! The director or the casting director wants to give the job to you. They are praying that you come in and make them stop breathing at the experience of watching you act. Take note, the casting people have had a long, hard day, and they have seen a lot of people who do not fit the bill, and when you walk in they are hungry to cast the part and move on to other matters. They are rooting for you. Do you get it? They are rooting for you!

"The bamboo that bends is stronger
than the oak that resists."

—Japanese proverb

~150~

I have an assignment for you. It is called the "Sleep Exercise." I want you to try this two times.

You are going to have a fantasy. First, choose an emotional direction, "in the extreme," for your fantasy. For instance, "the most exciting," or "the most enraging," or "the most delicious." You get the point? Whatever you decide, it must be in the extreme. Do not think about any details of the setup; simply choose the direction you want for your fantasy.

Next, set a timer for seven minutes and lie down in a quiet place where you will not be disturbed. Close your eyes, remind yourself of the direction for your fantasy, and then allow yourself, as best you can, to have a completely uncensored and non-steered fantasy. See if you can truly give up all control and let your fantasy lead you where it will. When the timer rings, open your eyes, and the fantasy is now over.

What we are working on here has to do with awareness of the mind's need to control. Remember to do this two times, each time choosing a different extreme direction for the fantasy.

"If you're in a bad situation, don't worry, it'll change. If you're in a good situation, don't worry, it'll change."

—John A. Simone Sr.

~151~

In the previous tip, I gave you an assignment called the "sleep exercise." Here is a report from True Acting Tips reader Wendy, a beginning acting student who lives in Auckland, New Zealand:

> I chose to have a fantasy that was in a direction of "the most wonderful," and I followed your directions to set a timer for seven minutes and then I got into bed as the sun was setting outside my window. When I closed my eyes, I suggested to myself that I wanted to have a most wonderful fantasy and then I took a deep breath and allowed the fantasy to begin. The first thing a saw in my

mind was my little sister's face smiling, and she was dancing, but then it started to rain on her and I started to think, "Wait, I don't want it to rain on her" and I tried to get rid of that image. Well, then I got really stuck in trying to come up with ideas that would make for a wonderful fantasy, and I had a very hard time allowing the fantasy to lead me rather them me leading it. This became quite frustrating, because the more I tried to allow the fantasy to be uncensored as you suggested, the more I found that I was controlling it. Then my timer started to ring and I realized that the seven minutes were over and I had spent most of the time in my head thinking about what a wonderful fantasy would be rather than actually having one! This was a revelation. and I really got an experience of how my mind gets in my way and I watch myself rather than getting involved.

Thanks, Wendy! Your experience really sums up the purpose of the sleep exercise, which is to become very aware of the mind's need to control your experience. The truth is that we all know how to fantasize, and in life we have fantasies all the time, but if they become uncomfortable, we usually stop ourselves from going any further.

In the Meisner technique, you are continually strengthening your "Actor's Imagination" so that you have the ability to be a fully creative artist, no longer hampered or sabotaged by the restrictions and censorship mechanisms of the mind. This means that you must become free to fantasize as you get in touch with what has profound meaning to you. Although all of the exercises we do in the Meisner approach are contributing to this process, when we get to emotional preparation, you learn more specifically how to access your most creative self. The sleep exercise was just a first step into this thrilling new world.

"When you finally go back to your old hometown, you find it wasn't the old home you missed but your childhood."

—Sam Ewing

~152~

I have the most wonderful and generous actors, directors, and teachers come to train with me in my Meisner Certificate Training Program, which I hold in the summers. It is my great pleasure to go back to the acting studio, class after class, in these intensive and rigorous four weeks.

Also, I have witnessed the way the students support each other as they face the huge demands of the work we do together. I was reminded of this quote from John Ruskin:

"In every person who comes near you look for what is good and strong, honor that; try to imitate it, and your faults will drop off like dead leaves when their time comes."

"We cannot live only for ourselves. A thousand fibers connect us with our fellow men."

—Herman Melville

~153~

Claude Bernard said:

"Man can learn nothing except by going from the known to the unknown."

For today, an important reminder.

Many actors try to stay in continual control of their performance. These actors, out of a deep fear of looking foolish, want to make sure that there are no surprises in store for them. This is one of the key reasons why many productions are general, riddled with cliché, and without life.

True Actors know that the unknown is the only place where true creation is possible. But to be willing, as well as physically and mentally able, to continually go where you don't know you're going, takes hard work, courage, and the hunger to be a creative artist.

> "I nod to a passing stranger, and the stranger nods back, and two human beings go off, feeling a little less anonymous."
>
> —Robert Brault

~154~

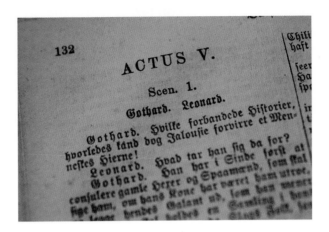

When you learn the lines of the script, it is very important to learn the words by rote. This means that you memorize the words without meaning so that you avoid locking yourself into any particular pattern of delivering your lines.

Once you have the words learned as best as you can and you think you really know them, here is a way to work with your partner to get the words even more planted into your veins, it is called a "line rehearsal."

Get a small ball or a pillow, anything you can toss back and forth with your acting partner. Stand about five feet apart and begin to throw the object back and forth rapidly. Then, as you are tossing the object to each other, begin to say the words of the scene as fast as you can. Spit the words out of your mouth mechanically, automatically, mindlessly, and without any pauses. If you take a pause to remember a word, you must start again at the beginning of the scene. If you get stuck and mess up a word, you must start again at the beginning of the scene. Continue to do this before every scene rehearsal until you can do the whole scene, from beginning to end, without any mistakes in the words and without any pauses.

In the line rehearsal, there is no acting, it is just words shooting out of your mouth as fast as possible. It is a great way to get stronger and stronger in really knowing the words. This is vital because when you put the scene on its feet, if you have a beautiful and unexpected moment between you and your partner, the first thing to go out the window will be the words, and when you get stuck in this way, you will both miss out on a wonderful opportunity of creation that was out of your control. But if you really know the words, they will simply ride on the wave of life that is happening and this creative event will take you by storm, which is exactly what we want.

"If you really put a small value upon yourself, rest assured that the world will not raise your price."

—Author unknown

~155~

In the Meisner technique, when you are first assigned a scene to work on, you are taught a very specific first step to working with your partner. This first reading of the scene is called a "Mechanical Reading." The name is most appropriate, because you read the words "syllable by syllable," slowly and in a relaxed way, without any inflection and without really beginning or ending the sentences. Also, at this point, you do not even look at your partner, you simply hear their voice, as they also read the words syllable by syllable.

If you try this, you will see that the mechanical reading makes it impossible to act! This is quite a revolutionary approach to working on the text. Many actors, out of a misunderstanding of the acting process, and pressured by directors who have no understanding of how to work with actors, attempt to give fully realized performances from the first read-through, which is of course impossible. For these actors, what they do on day one of rehearsals will be exactly what you will see them do when the play opens, throughout the run, and on closing night, with no growth or deepening.

With the mechanical reading as your very first step, the slowing down to read syllable by syllable gives your insides time to make personal connections with the role you are playing and in your relationship with the other actor. Because the meaning you are starting to find in the words is not yet permitted to be expressed, it keeps getting pointed back into your gut, where it will continue to "bake." This is a most important time to simply allow the meaning of the scene to take root in you without any pressure to do anything about it. The payoff will come very soon as you begin to put the scene on its feet.

"Every day we slaughter our finest impulses. That is why we get a heart-ache when we read those lines written by the hand of a master and recognize them as our own, as the tender shoots which we stifled because we lacked the faith to believe in our own powers, our own criterion of truth and beauty. Every man, when he gets quiet, when he becomes desperately honest with himself, is capable of uttering profound truths. We all derive from the same source. There is no mystery about the origin of things. We are all part of creation, all kings, all poets, all musicians; we have only to open up, to discover what is already there."

—Henry Miller

~156~

When you are handed your scene to work on in my acting classes, the first thing you are asked to do with your script is to rewrite it by hand, deleting all punctuation, capitals, and stage directions. Why do you think this is your first assignment? If you said it is because the punctuation, capitals, and stage directions lead your mind to a concept of how you should perform the text, you are right on the mark. If your mind sees an exclamation point, it thinks you need to get intense at the end of the sentence. If your mind sees a question mark at the end of a sentence, it thinks you must end the sentence by raising your inflection. By taking all the punctuation out, you take away the possibility for the mind to preconceive how the words should be delivered.

It is the same with stage directions. If the script says, "She told him with a gentle laugh in her eyes," your mind will try to produce a gentle laugh in your eyes at that moment. But what if that is not what is actually happening in your insides in that moment? Well, you will be obligated to fake it, which is what many actors do. This is called "illustrating the words," and it will lead you on a path to disaster in your performances.

The next time you work on a scene or on a play, try rewriting the script by hand and taking out all of the punctuation, capitals, and stage directions and discover the new freedom this gives you. Now you will begin to allow the words to emerge based on the life that is occurring between you and your partner! Sandy called this "the canoe on the river," where the "river" is the authentic life that is happening between two actors and the "canoe" is the text, which must ride freely on that life. Believe me, it is a breath of fresh air.

"No power in society, no hardship in your condition
can depress you, keep you down, in knowledge,
power, virtue, influence, but by your own consent."

—William Ellery Channing

~157~

Let's talk about imagination.

An important ingredient in the Meisner technique is the actor's imagination. In every step of the work, the ability to freely fantasize, without censorship or restriction, is being strengthened. Why is this so crucial? It is because the imagination is more persuasive then actual experience and it is a more organic and healthy way of working with your instrument.

Yes, I said healthy. When you work in this manner, because your insides know that the places you are going imaginatively to fulfill the demands of the script are not really happening, you can more fully embrace the circumstances you are creating and live them out "as if" they were true. We call this rare ability "actor's faith," or "the ability to fully accept the imaginary circumstances and live them out as if they were true."

Organic? Yes, this is so important. The use of your imagination, always aligned with an element of truth ("that which has actual meaning to you"), allows you to use what has deep meaning to you today. Personal meaning changes over time, so rather than trying to bring up experiences from the past as a source for emotional meaning, the use of your imagination always keeps you in the present and what has profound meaning to you right now. Take note, acting is an art of right now, right now, right now.

> "I have no special talents. I am only
> passionately curious."
>
> —Albert Einstein

~158~

Cotton Fitzsimmons said:

"You're not going to make me have a bad day. If there's oxygen on earth and I'm breathing, it's going to be a good day."

"The one real object of education is to have a man in the condition of continually asking questions."

—Bishop Mandell Creighton

~159~

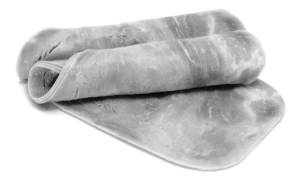

Out of the fear that they are not being "interesting," many actors fall into the trap of making things more than they actually are—more dramatic, more emotional, more powerful, more profound! But this attempt to convince the audience that more is happening than is actually happening is a lie. True Actors work with what is actually happening, no more and no less. This comes from trusting that the simple truth is enough.

"To lose one's self in reverie, one must be either very happy, or very unhappy. Reverie is the child of extremes."
—Antoine Rivarol

Here is an essay written by Roger Rosenblatt, which I found many years ago and which I always share with my students for the absolute power of its message. It is called, "I Am Writing Blindly."

Besides the newsworthy revelation of Lieut. Captain Dimitri Kolesnikov's dying message to his wife recovered last week from the husk of the sunken submarine Kursk—that 23 of the 118 crewmen had survived in an isolated chamber for a while, in contradiction to claims by Russian officials that all had perished within minutes of the accident—there was the matter of writing the message in the first place. In the first place, in the last place, that is what we people do—write messages to one another. We are a narrative species. We exist by storytelling—by relating our situations—and the test of our evolution may lie in getting the story right.

What Kolesnikov did in deciding to describe his position and entrapment, others have also done—in states of repose or terror. When a JAL airliner went down in 1985, passengers used the long minutes of its terrible, spiraling descent to write letters to loved ones. When the last occupants of the Warsaw Ghetto had finally seen their families and companions die of disease or starvation, or be carried off in trucks to extermination camps, and there could be no doubt of their own fate, still they took scraps of paper on which they wrote poems, thoughts, fragments of lives, rolled them into tight scrolls and slipped them into the crevices of the ghetto walls.

Why did they bother? With no countervailing news from the outside world, they assumed the Nazis had inherited the earth; that if anyone discovered their writings, it would be their killers, who would snicker and toss them away. They wrote because, like Kolesnikov, they had to. The impulse was in them, like a biological fact. So enduring is this storytelling need that it shapes nearly every human endeavor. Businesses depend on the stories told of past failures and successes, and on the myth of the mission of the company. In medicine, doctors increasingly rely on a patient's narrative of the progress of an ailment, which is inevitably more nuanced and useful than the data of machines. In law, the same thing. Every court case is a competition of tales told by the prosecutor and defense attorney; the jury picks the one it likes best.

All these activities derive from essential places in us. Psychologist Jerome Bruner says children acquire language in order to tell the stories that are already in them. We do our learning through storytelling processes. The man who arrives at our door is thought to be a salesman because his predecessor was a salesman. When the pattern-making faculties fail, the brain breaks down. Schizophrenics suffer from a loss of story. The deep proof of our need to spill, and keep on spilling, lies in reflex, often in desperate circumstances. A number of years ago, Jean-Dominique Bauby, the editor of Elle magazine in Paris, was felled by a stroke so destructive that the only part of his body that could move was his left eyelid. Flicking that eyelid, he managed to signal the letters of the alphabet, and proceeded to write his autobiography, The Diving Bell and the Butterfly, as the last grand gesture of his life.

All this is of acute and consoling interest to writers, whose odd existences are ordinarily strung between asking why we do it and doing it incessantly. The explanation I've been able to come up with has to do with freedom. You write a sentence, the basic unit of storytelling, and you are never sure where it will lead. The readers will not know where it leads, either. Your adventure becomes theirs, eternally recapitulated in tandem—one wild ride together. Even when you come to the end of the sentence, that dot, it is still strangely inconclusive. I sometimes think one writes to find God in every sentence. But God (the ironist) always lives in the next sentence.

It is this freedom of the message sender and receiver that connects them—sailor to wife, the dying to the living. Writing has been so important in America, I think, because communication is the soul and engine of democracy. To write is to live according to one's terms. If you ask me to be serious, I will be frivolous. Magnanimous? Petty. Cynical? I will be a brazen believer in all things. Whatever you demand I will not give you—unless it is with the misty hope that what I give you is not what you ask for but what you want. We use this freedom to break the silence, even of death, even when—in the depths of our darkest loneliness—we have no clear idea of why we reach out to one another with these frail, perishable chains of words. In the black chamber of the submarine, Kolesnikov noted, "I am writing blindly." Like everyone else.

"The walls we build around us to keep sadness out also keep out the joy."

—Jim Rohn

~161~

In an intellectual way, many actors choose external, physical gestures to reflect the nature of the character they are playing. Not going beyond the intellectual, they never arrive at anything related to the authentic expression of life itself. What these actors end up with is the cliché of character, indicated, representational, giving us their idea of the character rather than a living, breathing human being.

The True Actor understands that the route to authentic human behavior begins with a deep, personal connection to how the character sees the world.

Here's an investigation I would love you to try this week. I am going to give you a simple "character phrase" exercise that begins with a specific structure. The phrase holds within it two blank spaces. How you fill in these two blank spaces is the key to igniting your actor's imagination. Here's the structure of the phrase:

"I am a _____ in a world of _____s."

Let me give you an example so you get an idea of how this works. Let's say you fill in the blanks so that the phrase reads like this:

"I am a little sardine in a world of hungry sharks."

If you close your eyes and repeat that phrase to yourself for a few minutes, it just might start to give you an experience of how you see the world, and, if the images have some potency to you, it may even start to affect you viscerally and the world may begin to feel like a very scary place. Now, the more you freely fantasize with this phrase as the jumping-off place, the feelings that arise will begin to produce a physical life, as well. The way you look at people around you will become very specific; you may keep more distance between you and other people. If a stranger comes up to you and reaches out to shake your hand, you might discover that you refuse to return the handshake out of a fear that you will be gobbled up in some way, thinking, "What harm does this person have in mind for me!"

At the same time, if the choice of the words "sardine" and "sharks" has no meaning to you whatsoever, this particular phrase may just leave you cold.

As I said, your choice of words for the two blanks is vital. The words must have personal meaning to you and do something to your insides. Then, the more you work with the phrase you have constructed, the more you say it to yourself and fantasize freely, and the more you bring it into your rehearsals, the more you will begin to adopt the point of view the phrase points to. When this occurs, authentic physical behavior will happen all on its own.

"Don't do what you'll have to find an excuse for."

—Proverb

~162~

I would like you to examine something in your own life. What would it be like to only talk about those things you truly know? Try to find the times you offer opinions about things you actually have no direct experience of. I believe that if we all made this a practice, there would be a lot less talking and much more listening, and that's a very healthy thing, with the bonus of having a direct impact on your acting skills. Don't believe me—try it and see for yourself.

"Human beings, who are almost unique in having the ability to learn from the experience of others, are also remarkable for their apparent disinclination to do so."

—Douglas Adams

~163~

In acting class, there is no failure. Truly, every exercise you do, no matter how badly you think it goes, is planting the seed for your next breakthrough. If you can come to class with this attitude, you will gain a deeper relaxation, which is key to claiming the skills you are striving to learn. If you cannot recognize the truth in this, you will continually be your own worst critic and you may sabotage every attempt.

"As important as it is to keep picking yourself up and brushing yourself off, it's also important to stop tripping over your own two feet."

—Robert Brault

~164~

When Neo takes the red pill in The Matrix, he chooses to face a painful reality from which there is no turning back. Yet the difficult journey Neo commits to offers the only path toward aliveness and truth. I see the process of True Acting in the same light.

Early in your training, once you have witnessed your classmates having breakthroughs in class and, more importantly, once you have experienced getting fully out of your own way, you have also swallowed a pill after which your life will never be the same.

Yes, you may then choose to abandon these newly claimed values—I have seen some very gifted actors do it—but you will know that you have shrunk form doing your best work, and you will suffer for the missed opportunities. Isn't

A Path to Aliveness, Freedom, Passion, and Vitality • 297

this exactly what the character Cypher does in The Matrix when he chooses to betray Morpheus, Neo, and the others by striking a deal to be reinserted into the matrix? Oliver Wendell Holmes said:

"Man's mind, once stretched by a new idea, never regains its original dimensions."

"I have not failed. I've just found
10,000 ways that won't work."

—Thomas Edison

~165~

As True Actors, your clearest guideline is to live truthfully within the imaginary circumstances presented to you in the script. As you investigate the script, you are exploring the imaginary circumstances and how the character responds to them, in the most intimate way.

First and foremost, if you are going to examine the "character" of the person you are playing, it would be most useful to take a hard look at the circumstances you face in your own life and how you respond to them. Then you are strengthened to approach the playing of this role with a greater depth of understanding and humanity.

Here's a useful thought for actors from George Bernard Shaw:

"People are always blaming their circumstances for what they are. I don't believe in circumstances. The people who get on in the world are the people who get up and look for the circumstances they want and if they can't find them, make them."

"Fear is the cheapest room in the house. I would like to see you living in better conditions."

—Hāfez

~166~

In the Meisner technique, the acting student is trained first and foremost to be a fully receptive, available, and responsive human being, and this is worked on so rigorously that it becomes as natural as breathing. Now you have an actor who has the capacity to work in deep collaboration with a partner. It's a most intimate dance of being with each other, discovering each other anew, moment by moment by moment, and it is a great joy of our art.

Once again, this is where art reflects the truth of our lives. Read the way it was expressed by the Dalai Lama . . . "Consider the following. We humans are social beings. We come into the world as the result of others' actions. We survive here in dependence on others. Whether we like it or not, there is hardly a moment of our lives when we do not benefit from others' activities. For this reason it is hardly surprising that most of our happiness arises in the context of our relationships with others."

"I have accepted fear as a part of life, specifically the fear of change. I have gone ahead despite the pounding in the heart that says: turn back."

—Erica Jong

~167~

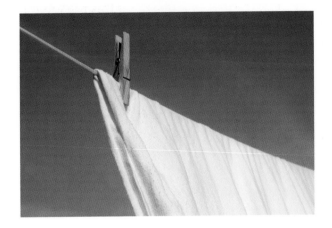

After enlightenment, the laundry.

"To forgive is to set a prisoner free and
discover that the prisoner was you."

—Lewis B. Smedes

~168~

Is achieving perfection your goal? Is it important to become the "perfect" actor? What does that even mean?

Here's a thought from Leonard Cohen:

"Ring the bells that still can ring, forget your perfect offering, there is a crack in everything, that's how the light gets in."

"A friend knows the song in my heart and sings it to me when my memory fails."

—Donna Roberts

~169~

A wonderful parable for your enjoyment and a smile:

God, seeing how desperately bored everyone was on the seventh day of creation, racked his over-stretched imagination to find something more to add the completeness he had just conceived. Suddenly his inspiration burst even beyond its own limitless bounds and he saw a further aspect of reality: its possibility to imitate itself. So he invented theater. He called his angels together and announced this in the following terms, which are still contained in an ancient Sanskrit document. "The theater will be the field in which people can learn to understand the sacred mysteries of the universe. And at the same time," he added with deceptive casualness, "it will be a comfort to the drunkard and to the lonely."

The angels were very excited and could hardly wait for there to be enough people on earth to put this into practice. The people responded with equal enthusiasm, and rapidly there were many groups all trying to imitate reality in their different ways. And yet the results were disappointing. What had sounded so amazing, so generous, and so all-embracing seemed to turn to dust in their hands. In particular, the actors, writers, directors, painters, and musicians couldn't agree amongst themselves as to who was the most important, and so they spent much of their time quarreling while their work satisfied them less and less.

One day, they realized they were getting nowhere and they commissioned an angel to go back to God to ask for help. God pondered for a long time. Then he took a piece of paper, scribbled on it, put it into a box, and gave it to the angel, saying, "Everything is here. This is my first and last word." The return of the angel to the theater circles was an immense event, and the whole profession crowded round him as the box was opened. He took out the parchment, uncurled it. It contained one word. Some read it over his shoulder, as he announced it to the others. "The word is 'interest.'"

"Interest?" "Interest!" "Is that all?" "Is that all?" There was a deep rumble of disappointment. "Who does he take us for?" "It's childish." "As if we didn't know . . ." The meeting broke up angrily, the angel left under a cloud, and the word, though never referred to again, became one of the many reasons for the loss of face that God suffered in the eyes of his creatures.

However, a few thousand years later, a very young student of Sanskrit found a reference to this incident in an old text. As he also worked part-time as a cleaner in a theater, he told the theater company of his discovery. This time, there was no laughter, no scorn. There was a long, grave silence. Then someone spoke. "Interest. To interest. I must interest. I must interest another. I can't interest another unless I'm interested myself. We need a common interest." Then another voice: "To share a common interest, we must exchange elements of interest in a way that's interesting . . ." ". . . to both of us . . ." "To all of us . . ." "In the right rhythm." "Rhythm?" "Yes, like making love. If one's too fast and one's too slow, it's not interesting . . ."

Then they began to discuss, seriously and very respectfully, what is interesting? Or rather, as one of them put it, what is really interesting? And here they disagreed. For some, the divine message was clear—"interest" meant only those aspects of living that were directly related to the essential questions of being and becoming, of God and the divine laws. For some, interest is the common interest of all men to understand more clearly what is just and unjust for mankind. For others, the very ordinariness of the word "interest" was a clear signal from the divine not to waste a moment on profundity and solemnity but just to get on with it and entertain. At this point the student of Sanskrit quoted to them the full text about why God created theater. "It has to be all these things at the same time, " he said. "And in an interesting way," added another. After which, the silence was profound.

They then began to discuss the other side of the coin, the appeal of the "uninteresting," and the strange motivations, social and psychological, that make so many people in the theater applaud so often and so vigorously what actually is of no interest to them whatsoever. "If only we could really understand this word . . ." said one.

> "I am convinced all of humanity is born with more gifts than we know. Most are born geniuses and just get de-geniused rapidly."
>
> —Buckminster Fuller

~170~

When you act, for your instrument to function effectively, you must be relaxed. I am not talking about being relaxed on just a physical level, which is vital, but there must also be a deep state of ease, a freedom from worry and constraint, a kind of liberation of the spirit that mobilizes in you a vitality and a readiness to take action.

"I resolve to speak ill of no man whatever, not even in a matter of truth; but rather by some means excuse the faults I hear charged upon others, and upon proper occasions speak all the good I know of everybody."
—Benjamin Franklin

A Path to Aliveness, Freedom, Passion, and Vitality • 309

~171~

Many actors never notice that they are thinking their way through the scene with their attention on themselves. It is vital that you become conscious of the moments you have left the scene and become "lost in thought."

Being lost in thought is dangerous in life, and it is equally dangerous on the stage.

Change comes only through awareness, and when you are aware that you are in your head thinking, where do you find the path back out? Your way out is always right over there in your partner and, out of your will, you must get your attention back on him or her. In this way, time after time, you will train yourself to stay present to what really matters.

"Feeling gratitude and not expressing it is like wrapping a present and not giving it."

—William Arthur Ward

Please remember that acting is doing something, doing something specific. Acting is not talking about, thinking about, or feeling about anything. It is very simple: if at any moment onstage you are not doing something specific, you are no longer acting. You are doing something that is unrelated to acting. If at any moment the director stops rehearsal and asks you what you are doing, you must be able to answer specifically. Moving from what is general to what is specific is your quest.

"Habit is habit, and not to be flung out of the window by any man, but coaxed downstairs a step at a time."
—Mark Twain

~173~

Curiosity: A strong desire to know or learn something.

Are you truly curious about the world around you and how people respond to it? It is not enough to go to acting class and work on your craft in the confines of the acting studio. Your classroom must be every place you walk and with every person you encounter along the way. They are your teachers. Ask questions and take notes.

The flip side of this coin is your exploration into the workings of your own mind and how you respond to the circumstances you are facing. This, too, is your classroom and key to deepening you craft, for your craft is not a technical device; it is a human one. As Ralph Waldo Emerson said . . . "He then learns that in going down into the secrets of his own mind he has descended into the secrets of all minds."

"True merit, like a river, the deeper it is, the less noise it makes."

—Edward Frederick Halifax

When a student is learning the Meisner foundation exercise called Repetition, one of the important first things the student will be told many times is to "take out the pauses." This is not about rushing or pace, and it has nothing to do with something you hear directors often tell actors: "Pick up your cues." (Which by the way, many directors misunderstand. Cues are not a technical element; they are determined by the actors' authentic need to respond.)

What is the reason for taking out the pauses in repetition? It is about strengthening the actors' ability to stay out of their heads as they become spontaneous responders to what other people are giving them, meaning, freely expressing how the other actors' behavior is impacting them. Here's a wonderful thing you can do. Next time you work on a scene with a partner, do a few rehearsals where you eliminate every pause. This will help you to not think your way through the scene, and it will lead to many new discoveries about the meaning of the material. When you get your head out of the way, you start to shift into the place where a deeper knowing can show up.

"In every real man a child is hidden that wants to play."
—Friedrich Nietzsche

~175~

I have written tips that are specifically about the craft of True Acting and others that are more philosophical and contemplative in nature. I hope you have enjoyed both types.

As I revisit some of my more technical tips, the ones that describe various ways of climbing inside the characters you play, I am aware that some actors may read these tips and say to themselves, "This looks time-consuming and demanding—is all this work really necessary?" Of course, for others, the hard work involved is very welcome and anticipated with pleasure.

Right now, I ask that you take some time to reflect on this question: "What is your heart's desire?" It is the intimate and honest answer to this question that will lead you forward on your own path of acting, for this desire is your fuel, your compass, and your anchor.

"To speak truly, few adult persons can see nature. Most persons do not see the sun. At least they have a very superficial seeing. The sun illuminates only the eye of the man, but shines into the eye and heart of the child. The lover of nature is he whose inward and outward senses are still truly adjusted to each other; who has retained the spirit of infancy even into the era of manhood."

—Ralph Waldo Emerson

~176~

Continuing from the previous tip, as you become more specifically acquainted with your true heart's desire, soak in
these words from Patrick Overton:

"When you come to the edge of all the light you know,
And are about to step off into the darkness of the unknown,
Faith is knowing one of two things will happen: There will
be something solid to stand on, Or you will be taught how
to fly."

"Character is much easier kept than recovered."

—Thomas Paine

~177~

True Actors are most fortunate; they stand on the stage and have a direct relationship with the people whose lives they are touching. Norman Rice said:

"Dare to reach out your hand into the darkness, to pull another hand into the light."

The sad part of so many jobs is that people never get to see the difference they ultimately make. The person who sits and puts little diodes into an iPod never sees the great enjoyment a person gets from listening to their music on the device.

When a play is really alive, meaning the actors live fully and authentically onstage, present to every moment, with great personal meaning and with tremendous passion in carrying out their mission, the audience does not want to leave when the show has concluded, and their applause does not mean that they have merely enjoyed themselves—it is actually a profound thank-you for bringing more light into their lives.

"Intuition is a spiritual faculty and does not explain, but simply points the way."

—Florence Scovel Shinn

~178~

In life, when you enter a room, are you coming from no-where? Of course not. In life, you are always coming from somewhere specific. The same is true onstage, yet many actors do not deal with this.

In the Meisner technique, when this first moment has an extreme emotional nature to it, you learn to fulfill this acting challenge with the technique called "emotional preparation." Of course, not every first moment has this extreme emotional component. Yet, as you learn to work imaginatively with yourself in the emotional-preparation exercises, you are also learning the basics of how to make your entrances specific and in alignment with the needs of the scene. Let's call it an emotional "warming up," because what has just happened to your character before the scene begins must have personal meaning to you the actor.

Again, not every entrance into a scene will be an extreme moment of the play, but it is always of importance, because there is no moment onstage that is casual. In fact, the word "casual" has no place in the actor's vocabulary! In the next tip, let's look a little more specifically at personalizing your entrance into the scene.

"Jealousy is simply and clearly the fear that you do not have value. Jealousy scans for evidence to prove the point that others will be preferred and rewarded more than you. There is only one alternative, self-value. If you cannot love yourself, you will not believe that you are loved. You will always think it's a mistake or luck. Take your eyes off others and turn the scanner within. Find the seeds of your jealousy, clear the old voices and experiences. Put all the energy into building your personal and emotional security. Then you will be the one others envy, and you can remember the pain and reach out to them."

—Jennifer James

~179~

In the previous tip, I talked about the fact that when we enter a room, we are always coming from somewhere specific and that the same must be true onstage; when you enter into a scene, you must also be coming from somewhere specific. Also, the place you are coming from must have personal meaning to you, the actor, and this is part of your job, to personalize the circumstances of the play.

I want to give you an example of how you might address the personalization of the circumstances the play gives you as you make an entrance into a scene.

Let's say that the character works at a gas station as a mechanic and he is coming home to his wife and kids from a tough day at work; he made a mistake on one of the cars he was working on and he had to rip out an expensive part he had installed. As he tried to get the part out, he accidentally cracked it and made it useless, and now, the boss is taking the cost of the part out of his paycheck, not good timing, as the dental bills for his daughter's braces are piling up and not getting paid. Obviously, as you make your entrance into the scene, your character is feeling rotten about his experience at work, which means that you, the actor, must also be feeling authentically rotten.

Well, the truth is, you are not a mechanic, you didn't ruin a repair job, and you don't have a daughter with braces. This is where you get to imaginatively personalize these circumstances so that they enable to you to fulfill the needs of this entrance. Here is a very simple example of how you might do this, by creating imaginary circumstances that are in alignment with the circumstances of the scene.

Let's say the truth is that you are new to acting, and to fund your acting classes, voice lessons, et cetera, you work at a hotel coffee shop part-time in the early morning shift, six days a week. We call this "the element of truth." There must be an element of truth, as it anchors the imaginary circumstances to your insides.

And another truth is that you don't like working at the coffee shop, but it has been tough finding jobs, and this one, at least, gives you the ability to go to classes and auditions. Also, with the minor salary and decent tips, financially, you are just getting by.

Now here's the imaginary part.

You just got your first agent! The agent is willing to represent you, and submit you for some upcoming pilots, but has demanded that you get professional headshots, which you have never had before. So, last week, you had a photo shoot with a top New York City photographer, and in order to get the digital files, you must first pay a hefty sum. This morning, at the coffee shop, you had four plates of sunny-side-up eggs on your arms, and as you served your customers, the eggs ran off of one of the plates and down a woman's very expensive dress, leaving it soaked in egg yolk. The manager had a meeting with you after your shift and told you that because of this incident, he was cutting you back from six shifts a week to two. Not good timing, as you were counting on the tips this week to pay for the digital files of your new headshots. This makes you feel just rotten!

You see, by creating imaginary circumstances that have true meaning to you, and by embracing these circumstances, you are brought to the experience of actually feeling rotten. Also, you can see how I constructed the imaginary circumstances so that they are in alignment with the circumstances of the play. They are not the same, but they are analogous and will help keep you related to the needs of the play.

Now, as you get ready to make your entrance, by fantasizing about your terrible day at the coffee shop and losing your chance to get submitted during pilot season by your new agent, you will now make your entrance coming from somewhere specific that actually has meaning to you. And as you enter into the scene, leaving the fantasy outside the door, the words you speak and all of your behavior will "ride on" the life that the personalization process has induced in you.

But listen very carefully.

Personalization is a rehearsal tool. The more you work with the imaginary circumstances in rehearsals, the more the meaning of these events will infiltrate and live within the speaking of the words and within all of your behavior. In other words, the meaning must become habitual so that you don't have to think about it anymore! Because the truth is, if you are thinking about these things onstage, you are no longer acting; you are in your head, unavailable to the life around you, and you are doing something unrelated to acting.

"If you want others to be happy, practice compassion. If you want to be happy, practice compassion."

—Dalai Lama

~180~

Here is a quote from Carl Jung:

"Nobody, as long as he moves about among the currents of life, is without trouble."

If we take a good look, we realize that suffering is something we all know. In acting classes, over the years, I have witnessed that 98 percent of actors have an easier access to their pain than to their joy, and this is why in creating acting exercises, most acting students will choose to use imaginary circumstances that are in the realm of "the most horrible and horrifying" rather than "the most exciting and wonderful."

The truth is, if you take a hard look at the wide scope of

dramatic literature, you will find that one of the key components in the journey of every character is suffering. Suffering is one of the building blocks in the story told by every script.

Here's an assignment. Look at some of your favorite play scripts or think about your most beloved movies and see that the element of suffering is the key to grasping the counterbalance to every character's deepest desire. Where there is desire, there is suffering. And there is always desire, for desire is inside the basic DNA of every human that walks the earth. It is also the seed for every character you will play.

> "Too often we underestimate the power of a touch, a smile, a kind word, a listening ear, an honest compliment, or the smallest act of caring, all of which have the potential to turn a life around."
>
> —Leo Buscaglia

~181~

The great truths speak to both our lives and to the art of True Acting at the same time. This is why, in my classes and here in the tips, I am continually relating acting to our lives—how we live our lives and the ways we operate as human beings. Without this connection, acting and all technique simply must be false. An anonymous quote I recently found makes for a perfect example:

"Remember, it's not your job to get people to like you; it's your job to like people."

You may say that you don't have to like everybody you meet, but then you are missing the point. The key here has to with "attention." It is a switch in attention from the continual concern for how you look and sound and what other people think of you, to giving your attention to others.

Can you see how this quote is calling for a willingness to spend less time staring at yourself in the mirror of life and more time becoming available to the other people in your world? Yes, it is the same for True Acting. It is the starting point.

So, let us all put the mirror aside each time it clouds our view and make the "attention on the other" a true practice.

"Remember that everyone you meet is afraid of something, loves something and has lost something."

—H. Jackson Brown Jr.

~182~

The inspiration for this tip comes from Nobel Prize winner André Gide, who said:

"One does not discover new lands without consenting to lose sight of the shore for a very long time."

If you currently in training to be a True Actor, or you are thinking of embarking on this path, this quote can serve you well.

Yes, absolutely, if you stay the course of your training, you will discover new lands in your ability to bring life to the stage, life with all its complexity, beauty, and continual surprises. You will also gain a new courage to be the complete expression of your deeper voice, your soul, your humanity, which is what makes you totally unique and different than any other actor who has stood on that stage.

Take note, the quote also makes clear that you must "consent to lose sight of the shore," and this is an insightful key to your training. Your willingness to return to the work every day, even when you cannot see clearly where it is taking you, will be tested many times. Only your true heart's desire will hold you steady. Are you prepared for this journey?

"One man cannot hold another man down in the ditch without remaining down in the ditch with him."

—Booker T. Washington

~183~

One of my great interests in teaching the craft of acting is making things less complicated. I do not mean that any of it is easy—it isn't—but we can certainly simplify things so that we have greater clarity.

Chopin said:

"Simplicity is the final achievement. After one has played a vast quantity of notes and more notes, it is simplicity that emerges as the crowning reward of art."

In my Meisner Certificate Program, we were discussing the acting term "beat." You have probably heard that word used quite often and maybe in many different ways. There is so much confusion about what a beat really is.

A beat is simply a "unit of action," no more and no less. Remember, in every moment onstage, the character is trying to accomplish something specific, and the beat is defined by this particular attempt. You might call this the "action" or the "objective," or the term I like to use, the "doing." Now, each time the character has a new objective or doing, that is the beginning of a new beat. See how this works?

Teachers and actors complicate the issue of beats in many ways. Some actors have been taught that they have to have a new beat with every line of the script. Craziness! This would drive you insane and make it impossible to act the part. Also, it is simply false.

As you learn the art of text analysis and interpretation, you will become deeply sensitized to what the character is really fighting for in every moment and how these struggles always relate back to his or her deepest desire. Breaking the script down into beats is like locating the buoys in the sea; beats simply help you stay on target as you navigate through the many obstacles the play presents.

One last thing. When you break the script down into beats, you must also be aware of something called "adjustments," and I will discuss this in the next tip.

"The purpose of life is a life of purpose."

—Robert Byrne

~184~

In the previous tip, I defined the acting term "beat" as a unit of action, what the character is fighting for specifically, which we call the character's objective or "doing." And when there is a change in what the character is trying to accomplish, this is the beginning of a new beat.

I also mentioned that you will need to know what an "adjustment" is so that, as you look at the script, you are able to make a distinction between a change in the beat or when the beat simply continues as the character adjusts to what the other characters are doing and to what is happening in the world around him.

Here's a simple example . . .

Let's say that you are doing a scene between a mother and daughter and you are playing the mother. The circumstances are that your daughter, who is sixteen and does not have her driver's license yet, took your car keys last night while you were sleeping and drove your car over to her best friend's house. After she picked up her friend, they picked up more of their friends and went to the Dairy Queen. While they were driving around, eating ice cream and blasting the radio, your daughter drove off the side of the road and hit a telephone pole. The kids were okay, except for one of the friends, who had minor cuts and bruises. Your car was not so lucky—it has major damage to the front end.

In the scene between you and your daughter, you have determined that the beat begins right at the top of the scene with you sitting next to your daughter on the living room sofa, and it ends when your daughter runs out of the room crying. You have also phrased your objective or "doing" in these words: "to teach her a lesson she will never forget."

Imagine beginning your speech, warning your daughter that she must never do this again and that the ramifications of her actions will be severe and how she could have killed herself or one of her friends! At first, she sits very still and listens to your words, but suddenly she closes her eyes and puts her hands over her ears. Some actors would call this a new beat. It is not a new beat, it is simply an adjustment. Your intention and objective is still to "teach her a lesson she will never forget," but how you actually teach the lesson must change as you adjust to the new behavior you are receiving from your partner. Then your daughter starts to hit you; you must adjust once again. Then she wraps her arms around you and cries, and again you adjust. Finally, she leaps to her feet and runs out of the room and the beat ends. See? We have one beat with a number of adjustments.

This lesson also gives you important information about how you must work with an objective. Yes, you can figure out the objectives when you are doing your homework on the script, but how you do the objective is always given to you by your partner. So the "how you do what you are doing" is discovered in your working with the other actors! All right, get a scene and a partner and go have some fun.

"For if there is a sin against life, it consists perhaps not so much in despairing of life as in hoping for another life and in eluding the implacable grandeur of this life."

—Albert Camus

~185~

Let's continue with our theme of the character's "objective" or, as I have mentioned, what I like to call the "doing."

In the previous tip, I told you that "how you do what you are doing" is discovered in your working with the other actors. To be very clear, this means that once you have determined what the objective or doing is, you must uncover the ways of doing it "in the doing of it" rather than "in the thinking about it."

This True Acting truth goes against how many actors work on an objective, which is to pre-plan their every move. But pre-planning leaves out the most important of all acting ingredients, your acting partners!

To be willing to discover "how to do what you are doing in the doing of it" requires the courage to go where you do not know you are going and to bring forth all of your creative resources. It also requires taking risks and being willing to explore freely with your mind, body, and spirit. Remember, the objective must be accomplished with all of your behavior, which includes the speaking of the words, your physical and emotional behavior, and the way you listen and receive what the other actors are giving you.

Once you have become an actor who has the ability to fully receive every nuance of your partners' behavior and then respond to their behavior through the specific lens of what you are trying to accomplish, only then can you actually know if you are getting closer to realizing your deeply held desire in the play. Are you achieving the objective? You will see it in your partner! Are you losing the battle? You will see it in your partner! In every moment, it is your partner who tells you if you are winning or not. Your job is to allow that information to tell you what the next necessary course of action will be.

"The miracle is not to fly in the air, or to walk on the water, but to walk on the earth."

—Chinese proverb

~186~

Here is a quote from an unknown author:

"There are no guarantees. From the view of fear, none are strong enough. From the viewpoint of love, none are necessary."

When you get cast in a role, my suggestion is to enjoy the moment and appreciate the fact that the people who have their lives invested in this project have decided that you are valuable, reliable, and gifted. The key here is to "enjoy the moment" and then get to work. Let me clarify this point with this ancient zen story . . .

There lived an old farmer who had worked on his fields for many, many years. One day, his horse bolted away. His neighbors dropped in to commiserate with him. "What awful luck," they tut-tutted sympathetically, to which the farmer only replied, "We'll see."

Next morning, to everyone's surprise, the horse returned, bringing with it three other, wild horses. "How amazing is that!" they exclaimed in excitement. The old man replied, "We'll see."

A day later, the farmer's son tried to mount one of the wild horses. He was thrown on the ground and broke his leg. Once more, the neighbors came by to express their sympathies for this stroke of bad luck. "We'll see," said the farmer politely.

The next day, the village had some visitors—military officers who had come with the purpose of drafting young men into the army. They passed over the farmer's son, thanks to his broken leg. The neighbors patted the farmer on his back—how lucky he was to not have his son join the army! "We'll see," was all that the farmer said.

As a onetime devoted basketball player, I enjoy watching some of my favorite NBA teams, but I always cringe when I see a player make a basket and then spend so much time celebrating and high-fiving another player that the opposing team goes right by him and scores an easy layup. Please,

please, please, play the game and save the celebrating for when the game is over. This is also very much like the players who tell the media at the press conference the day before the big game that they guarantee a victory for their team. Of course, these promises do not always come to fruition. Please, just play the game.

When you have been cast in a production, there is no guarantee about anything, really. The producers may run out of money and the whole thing may come to a halt. The director may get pressure from the producers to replace you if they are not pleased with the progress of rehearsals. The show may open on Thursday night and close before the next performance. Of course, the flip side of this coin is also possible and you may get the greatest reviews ever received by an actor in that particular role. Who knows!

So play the game fully and leave it all on the court. And by "play the game" I mean, get down to the work at hand, get out your script, and begin the process of injecting those words with life. Trust that a time for celebration will come.

"Having spent the better part of my life trying either to relive the past or experience the future before it arrives, I have come to believe that in between these two extremes is peace."

—Author unknown

~187~

The theme for this tip comes from this wonderful zen quote:
"Great faith. Great doubt. Great effort. The three qualities necessary for training."

The message in these words needs to be taken to heart by anyone considering walking the path of True Acting.

Yes, first you must begin with great faith, a faith that your heart's desire is leading you in the right direction, a faith in your teacher and that she or he has your best interests in mind, a faith that the particular technique of acting you are studying is going to be healthy and useful.

Then, invariably, if you are in a process that is challenging your habitual ways of behaving and thinking, you will arrive at a place where you will face great doubt that you have any talent whatsoever or that you can persevere. The difficulty at this point is that the bleakness may be so dark that the light of the faith you began with has become hidden from view. But there is a way forward.

The way forward is always with great effort. This means that no matter how you are feeling, your saving grace will be to continue to work hard. Truly, this is the only way to uncover the faith that has been at your side all along. Only relentless effort, under the tremendous internal pressure you are experiencing, will give you the ultimate strength to create freely and joyfully.

As a teacher, my main requirement is that my students be willing to work very hard because I know that, if they do, they will grow. The question you must ask yourself? Are you willing to work this hard even though it may not always be comfortable? Please reflect on that.

"Nothing ever gets anywhere. The earth keeps turning round and gets nowhere. The moment is the only thing that counts."

—Jean Cocteau

~188~

In the Meisner technique, you learn how to build something from the ground up. The basic exercises continually grow, with new elements being added step by step, until the exercise contains all of the dramatic elements you will encounter in a script. So, in every step of this process, you are being prepared to work on text and character.

Sandy was brilliant in this way; he knew that the worst thing you can do to an acting student in the very beginning is give them a script to work on. He was wise enough to create an approach that says, first and foremost, we must have a fully functioning, alive, receptive, and spontaneously expressive human being.

The work presses you right up against your own mind, which desperately wants to control. Here, a deep level of frustration sets in as you begin to understand that the mind cannot solve the challenges of the work. For those who stick with it, going through the pain of this profound frustration and feelings of hopelessness, they discover a new power and clarity in their work that they never dreamed was possible.

Early on in the process, I always tell students that whatever they imagine or think this work is about, I promise that it is greater than that. Down the road, for those who have relentlessly applied themselves to the practice, they find that this is absolutely true.

"Pour some water into a tub and stir it up. Now try as hard as you can to calm the water with your hands; you will succeed in agitating it further. Let it stand undisturbed a while, and it will calm down by itself. The human brain works much the same way."

—Koichi Tohei

~189~

It is useful to remember that the training of an actor begins with reenergizing the abilities you were born with, the very things that make you most human.

I hope this will be encouraging to you, because what I am saying is that you already possess everything you need and you do not need to look outside of yourself for anything more. Breathe that one in.

As Pablo Picasso said:

"Every child is an artist. The problem is how to remain an artist once he grows up."

"Never say, "oops." Always say, "Ah, interesting."

—Author unknown

~190~

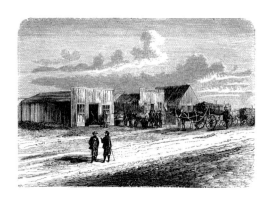

Consider each performance of the play you are in to be another rehearsal.

This means, continually risk going where you have not ventured before. If you are fortunate, you will be working with other actors who are willing and able to go on that wonderful roller-coaster ride called "the unknown" with you.

What a thrill for the audience to see actors work in this way. What a joy to work in a company of actors who relish this ongoing exploration of the play. Look at the truth of our lives:

"Your current safe boundaries were once unknown frontiers."

"Passion is universal humanity. Without it religion, history, romance and art would be useless."

—Honoré de Balzac

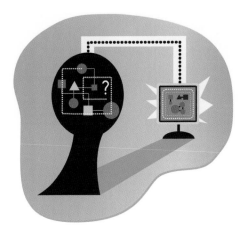

Do not mix up truth with technique; they are two very different things.

Technique, if it is valid, will open the gateway for you to become the expression of truth. Technique, if it is not valid, will merely add more data to your brain. As Madeleine L'Engle said: "Truth is eternal, knowledge is changeable. It is disastrous to confuse them."

"Patience and perseverance have a magical effect before which difficulties disappear and obstacles vanish."

—John Quincy Adams

~192~

No matter which direction you aim for, there is no controlling this thing called a "career" as an actor. The truth is that your career will find you. Your job is to keep working at your craft, whether it is on the stage, in front of the camera, or in the acting studio; keep working.

As you learn to take your attention off of the results and stay in the enjoyment of the moment, you may be surprised to realize one day that a career has made its claims on you. Gary Sinise said:

"Careers, like rockets, don't always take off on schedule. The key is to keep working the engines."

"If we have no peace, it is because we have forgotten that we belong to each other."

—Mother Teresa

~193~

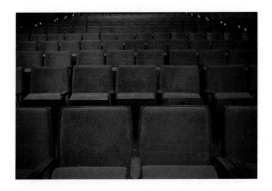

Theater is an art of "being witnessed." This is why the act of theater doesn't really happen until the audience arrives. Of course, this is a reflection of a basic life truth, that one of our deepest and most human desires is to have our lives witnessed.

If you have been around little children, you will hear them call out, over and over, "Mommy look at me do this, watch me, watch me, watch me do this, Mommy look, look at this, watch me do this!" This is a desire that never fades.

Isn't this an important key to what is driving you up onto the stage?

> *"You see, when weaving a blanket, an*
> *Indian woman leaves a flaw in the weaving*
> *of that blanket to let the soul out."*

> —Martha Graham

~194~

As a person striving to reach this space in your work we are calling True Acting, you will be inviting harsh criticism into your life, not from your audience—they come fully willing and ready to fall in love with you—but from other actors.

Sadly, there will be times when the fierce negativity you encounter will be from the very people who are supposed to be your partners onstage. As best you can, stay calm and clear, as these particular people have a toxic mindset. Understand that their lives are devoted to tearing you down in the attempt to raise themselves up. Do not buy in to the sickness these frightened little people spread; make no comment on it. There is no need to defend yourself, and their attacks have less weight than hot air. Keep doing your work, and the world will see and take care of the rest for you.

> "If one dream should fall and break into a
> thousand pieces, never be afraid to pick one
> of those pieces up and begin again."
>
> —Flavia Weedn

~195~

There will be times when you are cast in the part of a character that you do not really like; you do not like this person and you are hesitant to spend this much of your time with him or her. This is an important signal to pay attention to.

What do you do?

Most importantly, take a big breath and pause. Read the script a few more times before making any major decisions. Then ask yourself if you can find a way to fall in love with this person, which simply must happen if you are going to be able to work effectively.

Start by asking questions. Has the person been damaged in any ways that you can relate to? What really is behind this character's behavior, and what are they longing for? What are the roots of their suffering, and where do they find joy? If you can begin to touch these things in a personal way, you may discover the path toward enjoying yourself in this particular role.

"If we are facing in the right direction, all we have to do is keep on walking."

—Buddhist saying

~196~

In acting terms, I like to call it the "deeper wish," the very thing that is driving the character to make the choices he makes and take the actions he takes. It is the most fundamental and intimate part or our being; it is the core of humanity. As Khalil Gibran said:

"To understand the heart and mind of a person, look not at what he has already achieved, but at what he aspires to."

"When a man sits with a pretty girl for an hour, it seems like a minute. But let him sit on a hot stove for a minute and it's longer than any hour. That's relativity."

—Albert Einstein

~197~

The True Actor learns specific ways to look inside oneself, to reflect on the workings of the human instrument in a most intimate way. This must come first, as it opens the eyes to see clearly in every direction. Elias Canetti said:

"The self-explorer, whether he wants to or not, becomes the explorer of everything else. He learns to see himself, but suddenly, provided he was honest, all the rest appears, and it is as rich as he was, and, as a final crowning, richer."

"Take your life in your own hands, and what happens? A terrible thing: no one to blame."

—Erica Jong

~198~

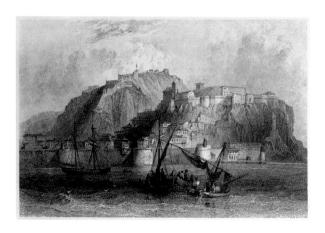

When you care about every moment, when you are willing to struggle to make every choice ring true, when you fight to realize your vision in partnership with the team around you, you bring a level of quality to the production that will then make a difference to the community of people who come to see the play. Reminds me of this old quote:

"In communities where men build ships for their own sons to fish or fight from, quality is never a problem."

"God has entrusted me with myself."

—Epictetus

~199~

As you continue your studies, there will be times when you feel hopelessly stuck and you think you are making no progress whatsoever. The main thing you must do in these moments is to continue to do the work. As Ovid said:

"What is harder than rock, or softer than water? Yet soft water hollows out hard rock. Persevere."

"Remember, we all stumble, every one of us.
That's why it's a comfort to go hand in hand."
—Emily Kimbrough

~200~

Of course we are all indebted to the transformative work of Constantin Stanislavski. Here's some advice from him to all of us:

"The actor must recreate his work, each time he repeats his part, with sincerity, truth and directness. It is only on that condition that he will be able to free his art from mechanical and stereotyped acting, from 'tricks' and all forms of artificiality. If he accomplishes this, he will have real people and real life all around him on the stage, and living art which has been purified from all debasing elements."

"Oh, the comfort, the inexpressible comfort of feeling safe with a person, having neither to weigh thoughts nor

measure words, but pouring them all right out, just as they are, chaff and grain together; certain that a faithful hand will take and sift them, keep what is worth keeping, and then with the breath of kindness blow the rest away."

—Dinah Craik

~201~

When you audition for a play, do a few things many actors simply do not do.

Learn as much as you can about the theater, the director, and the season of plays that the theater is producing, and go to the audition with a real interest in learning more.

Also, please take the time and make the effort to read the entire play. Even though you may be auditioning with a monologue, you just might be handed sides to read with another actor at the audition, or the director may ask how you "see" the character you are auditioning for, so be prepared for these unexpected opportunities.

"The greatest explorer on this earth never takes voyages as long as those of the man who descends to the depth of his heart."

—Julien Green

~202~

Having authentic feelings onstage is not enough; they must be the fuel for you to take action. The two must always work in partnership: your honest emotional responses and then what you actually do.

Feelings alone lead to a mushy, general, and self-absorbed performance. Action alone is intellectual, indicated, and representational.

"It is only when we silence the blaring sounds of our daily existence that we can finally hear the whispers of truth that life reveals to us, as it stands knocking on the doorsteps of our hearts."

—K. T. Jong

~203~

One of the great joys in the craft of True Acting occurs as your imagination is set free. Here, in our closing tip, I thought it would be useful and fun for you to hear how others, throughout time, have looked at the imagination as a fundamental human, creative force:

"A rock pile ceases to be a rock pile the moment
a single man contemplates it, bearing
within him the image of a cathedral."
—Antoine de Saint-Exupéry

"All men who have achieved great things
have been great dreamers."

—Orison Swett Marden

"Everything that is new or uncommon raises a pleasure
in the imagination, because it fills the soul with an
agreeable surprise, gratifies its curiosity, and gives
it an idea of which it was not before possessed."

—Joseph Addison

"Fiction reveals truths that reality obscures."

—Jessamyn West

"I am imagination. I can see what the eyes
cannot see. I can hear what the ears cannot
hear. I can feel what the heart cannot feel."

—Peter Nivio Zarlenga

"I believe in the imagination. What I cannot see is
infinitely more important than what I can see."

—Duane Michals

"I doubt that the imagination can be suppressed.
If you truly eradicated it in a child, he
would grow up to be an eggplant."

—Ursula K. Le Guin

"I like nonsense, it wakes up the brain cells. Fantasy is a necessary ingredient in living, it's a way of looking at life through the wrong end of a telescope. Which is what I do, and that enables you to laugh at life's realities."

—Dr. Seuss

"I paint objects as I think them, not as I see them."

—Pablo Picasso

"I saw the angel in the marble and carved until I set him free."

—Michelangelo

"Imagination and fiction make up more than three quarters of our real life."

—Simone Weil

"Imagination grows by exercise, and contrary to common belief, is more powerful in the mature than in the young."

—W. Somerset Maugham

"Imagination has brought mankind through the dark ages to its present state of civilization. Imagination led Columbus to discover America. Imagination led Franklin to discover electricity."

—L. Frank Baum

"Imagination is the voice of daring. If there is anything Godlike about God it is that. He dared to imagine everything."

—Henry Miller

"Imagination will often carry us to worlds that never were. But without it we go nowhere."

—Carl Sagan

"Live out of your imagination, not your history."

—Stephen Covey

"Our truest life is when we are in dreams awake."

—Henry David Thoreau

"People who lean on logic and philosophy and rational exposition end by starving the best part of the mind."

—William Butler Yeats

"Personally, I would sooner have written Alice in Wonderland than the whole Encyclopedia Britannica."

—Stephen Leacock

"Some stories are true that never happened."

—Elie Wiesel

"The imagination is man's power over nature."

—Wallace Stevens

"The man who has no imagination has no wings."

—Muhammad Ali

"There are no rules of architecture
for a castle in the clouds."

—Gilbert K. Chesterton

"There is a boundary to men's passions when
they act from feelings; but none when they
are under the influence of imagination."

—Edmund Burke

Your assignment? Have a wonderful and delightful fantasy.
Or maybe two!

"I may not have gone where I intended to go, but I
think I have ended up where I intended to be. "

—Douglas Adams

Part Two

True Actor Resources

Dr. Richard Kowal on Finding Your Sharpest Edge

Like a carpenter who must keep his cutting blades sharp or a painter whose brushes must always be kept clean and supple, you are a craftsman whose tools must be maintained at the highest level.

The most attractive quality in a person is their enthusiasm for life. We can feel it in others, and others feel it in us. A palpable state of enthusiasm requires energy and vitality. Do you have enough? Have you done everything possible to max out your energy, vitality, and enthusiasm? If not, is there a way to amp up your energy today, right now?

Diet is the most fundamental strategy for improving your well-being. The right dietary approach can bring us limitless energy, a perfect body composition, and wonderful mental clarity. And the beauty of dietary strategies is that you don't need to add a new discipline to your life; you're already eating!

Try this simple test to see whether your diet is supporting your vitality and mental focus:

1. I often experience a general sense of fatigue.
2. It's not unusual for me to have a period of mental confusion, for example, "I'm not sure what I should be doing right now."
3. It is not unusual for me to feel an "energy dropout" at some point during the day, especially when I come back

from lunch.

4. I can get irritable if I miss a meal or if I have to put off eating.

If any of these statements sounds familiar, then dietary strategies will bring a major improvement in your energy and the quality of your mental focus. Why do dietary choices make such an impact on your energy level?

Imagine that you're camping out and starting a campfire. First you gather thin sticks of dry kindling. These will burn hot, high, and fast. Then, over the kindling, you put a large, dense log of hardwood, such as oak. The hardwood log won't burn as hot or as fast as the kindling wood, but it will burn steadily and for a long time. Protein is like hardwood; a good portion will give you consistent energy and mental focus for hours. Baked goods, cereal and juice, which are carbohydrates, are like kindling. This type of energy is too short-lasting to get you through your morning with consistent mental focus. You have to load up your fire with hardwood to burn steadily throughout the morning.

This is how you begin:

1. Start your day with adequate protein. This could be an egg omelet (whites only for those with higher cholesterol) with veggies or low-fat cheese; low-fat cottage cheese and berries; or even leftover chicken, salmon, or steak from last night's dinner. (A portion the size of a deck of cards, or about four ounces, is fine.)

2. If you need to snack between breakfast and lunch, or lunch and dinner, then snack. But again, put a log of hardwood onto your fire, not kindling. In other words, avoid

muffins, cake, and candy. Try a protein drink or protein bar of your choice. (These should have between 150 and 220 calories.) These are widely available and easy to obtain. Alternatively, a piece of low-fat cheese or a small serving of low-fat cold cuts will serve the same purpose.

3. For lunch, try going light. A heavy, fatty meal (burgers, fries, soda) will fill you but will also put you in a lower energy state following lunch. Your mind will be slow and you will lose enthusiasm and focus. Not good for auditions or acting. Try a hearty salad with a serving of chicken, fish, or egg salad. Trade your soda for seltzer. Skip the bread and dessert. It's okay if you're not full to the brim. Risk it and see how you feel when you're back at work. You'll feel lighter, more energetic, and more focused.</NL>

If you honestly try these strategies, you'll feel more energy and less fatigue during the first week, perhaps even the first day. Remember, you are responsible for your own state. A wise old actor once said to me, "Just catch on fire about what you're doing and people will come from miles around to watch you burn!"

What follows is a quick guide for implementing a Power Eating strategy for the following week.

Power Eating for Actors

Breakfast Three-egg omelet with veggies or low-fat cheese (whites only if you have high cholesterol, i.e., over 220), and skip the home fries and the bread. Coffee is fine, but limit the sugar, and no fruit juice.

Midmorning or midafternoon snack, and only if needed A protein bar with 15 grams or more of protein and 15 grams or less of total carbohydrate. A protein drink with a similar ratio of protein to carb is also fine. A widely available soy drink is Silk brand vanilla. (Added bonus, soy protein lowers cholesterol!)

Lunch Cold-cut sandwich with 4 ounces of low-fat cold cuts (white-meat poultry is best); throw away the top piece of bread—one slice is fine. Or, a generous green salad topped with 4 ounces of tuna salad, grilled chicken, or salmon. Still hungry? Have more salad, but not more protein, and skip the bread, juice, and potatoes (if it's crunchy and comes in a plastic bag, don't have it.) Dessert: not until dinner, as it will tire you out for the whole afternoon.

Dinner Green salad, as much as you want; olive oil and vinegar is the best dressing; 4-6 ounces of low-fat protein such as fish, poultry, or occasionally lean red meat. High-water-content vegetables such as broccoli, cauliflower, Brussels sprouts, kale, chard, unlimited. (Really, any veggies except the high-starch potatoes, corn, peas, carrots, artichoke, or winter squash.) Dessert: three or four times a week.

Wine/beer/alcohol? More than a glass a night and you'll feel it on the following day.

It is clear that if you are on a mission to become the best actor you can be, you need to create a reservoir of energy, vitality. and well-being that will support you through all the challenges that you will face along the way.

Dr. Richard Kowal has been practicing science-based clinical nutrition for over twenty-five years. He has appeared on numerous television news programs, including on NBC, CBS, and Fox, and has also been interviewed by many magazines, including New York Magazine, Men's Vogue, *and* USA Today, *for comments regarding health and wellness. He is the author of* The Skinny Book of Weight Loss Tricks *(www.skinnytricks.com) and works with actors and performers throughout the country to make vibrant living and weight loss an achievable goal. You can reach Dr. Kowal in his New York office at 212.799.2520.*

Artotems Co. on the New Art of Promotion

If people don't know about you, you won't be found. If people can't find you, you won't be contacted. Simple truths.

As most of consumers know, a sea change has occurred in how we communicate and how we must promote what we do if we expect to succeed. While the phone and letters are still valid forms of communication, they require an extra effort that many busy recipients don't have time for and relegate to the circular file. What they make time for is the web. Whether it's email, search, or social media, that's where contact now occurs. With this change, even traditional outlets of promotion using print ads struggled to adapt to digital consumption of what they have to say. They know they must evolve. Demographics for that consumption clearly show that if you want to be seen and heard by a very large part of potential audiences, the place to start is online. Whether you are a company creating widgets or an actor performing drama, welcome to the new boat. We are all in it together.

As an artist you want your efforts to be seen. In the past, others often controlled how you were seen. That, too, has changed. As a creative individual, you can now promote your own work in ways that are powerful and reach a worldwide audience. You can shape and control the presentation of your efforts. You can reach out and develop an audience. Chances are, if you create it, there is an audience out there for it. What does it take to do this?

Time, effort, and access to basic computer technology are all that is necessary to begin.

Ah, time! If only we had more of it. Our good friend the artist Steve Muhs has this to say about promoting his work: "I know I need to do it, but I don't want to stop working to do it. If I don't, though, then who am I making the art for? Who will see it?" His concern and his questions are valid. Like a lot of creative people, for him time is an issue. His work is demanding and requires a great deal of attention, and yet it still must be seen in order to be experienced and appreciated. He also adds that it "feels odd" to promote himself and his work. Our response is this: If you owned a company that produced a good product, would you be hesitant to promote it? Of course you wouldn't. If you don't do it, who will? As an actor you are essentially running your own business. It, like other businesses, must be marketed. And like other businesses, it has competition. However, as an actor the products you produce are unique because they are creative expressions from within you. Martha Graham, the dancer, had this to say about creative expression:

"There is a vitality, a life force, an energy, a quickening, that is translated through you into action, and because there is only one of you in all time, this expression is unique."

Finding an outlet for others to see and hear your unique talent is essential, so the time and effort are worthwhile. Whether you do it yourself or find an individual or organization to help, the online resources are out there and free to use. Let's take a look at a few.

Online Promotion Essentials

Online promotion comes in many forms. Today's basics are these.

Website

Your website is the basic container/package of what you want to promote. Websites come in many shapes and styles. How you style your container is essential to your message. If you have a built-in audience who knows your product and is out there searching for it, the container can look like practically anything. If you don't, your message needs to be front and center, and the container needs to be somewhat transparent. It's our view that simplicity is essential. Viewers of websites usually don't stick around if they can't find what they are looking for very quickly. The content of a home page on a website must be informative, enticing, and valuable to the viewer. As the great architect and designer Charles Eames said, "The details are not the details. They make the design." Your details (specific content) are the key to promotion. You typically have only a moment to make your point. Being clear and succinct are important to getting your message across. Your viewers want to know as quickly as possible if they can't find what they are looking for. Chances are, they arrived at your site because of search efforts (an area that is practically a book in itself) or because they engaged with something in reference to you online. That "something," these days, is often a post done in a social media online venue or elsewhere.

Social Media

Being engaged with social media venues has two very real benefits. It builds your audience/fan base and also has an impact on your searchability within online search engines. Your frequency of using these venues and how you use them can have a tremendous impact on your online visibility. Let's take a look at the most frequently used social-media venues that we have found to be very effective.

Twitter: Within the space of 140 characters, you can send out your messages to the world. With this length constraint, Twitter has a way of making people get to the point of what they have to say. Including both a message and a link to what matters to you can be a powerful promotional tidbit.

Facebook: Facebook can be used for longer messages, with images, links, video, and notes about your content. With all the news about Facebook, who hasn't heard something about it? That, in and of itself, makes it important. It's a venue for both personal and business-related content. Typically a business page is created for the purpose of promoting something; however, more and more people are using personal pages for this, as well. We think caution is called for when using a personal page to promote your professional efforts. Much of what is posted on a personal page isn't really suited for promotion.

Flickr: Flickr is a place for your images, screenshots, and short videos. Each piece of content can be titled, described, and tagged (a way of helping search engines find it) to promote what you do. As the old saying goes, an image is worth a thousand words. In the case of Flickr, you can use both images and words.

This powerful combination is a highly effective mix for search engines.

YouTube: The mantra for promotion lately is video, video, and more video. Consuming video has become a hot online activity. YouTube is a place for all kinds of video. A good video can go a long way toward promoting what you do. If it's titled, described, and tagged correctly, it can rise in search with greater frequency than some other types of content.

Google: Although a newcomer to the social media world, Google+ may be an important player soon. Let's not forget where most people begin online searches. Yep, it's Google, and posts in Google+ get into search. Only time will tell how important this tool will be.

While many other avenues exist, we see those five as good places to start online promotion.

Perception

As you explore these venues and create posts, keep a few things in mind.

When that post goes out, how will it be perceived? Is the intention clear? Our policy is to check and double-check everything we post. It's a good idea to write down clearly what you want to present as you begin using social media. Ask a few questions as you do this: Will viewers learn something new from my posts? Will they be amused? Will my posts spark an interest in them? Will they upset anyone? We post a lot of items for a diverse group of businesses. We have to know their intentions and their products, and we can't really bring our own thoughts and feelings into the mix. As is the case with all communication, there are some things to avoid if we want stay clear of problems.

Oops

As humans we have a tendency to sometimes get sidetracked into our personal thoughts and feelings. We all have biases, and those don't really belong as part of a marketing package. They can distract from an intended message in ways that only show up later. As we have watched public figures using social media, we have seen some very striking blunders when things have been said and biases have been made obvious. These "slips" have created very real problems for them. Remember, posting something and deleting it doesn't make it go away. The web is a collective, and people collect those mistakes despite best intentions and the delete function. In spite of this warning, what you post does need to matter to you to be effective. If it doesn't, that becomes clear to your audience.

Social Means Social

Social media isn't a TV or magazine ad. Your enthusiasm and inspirations can be vital to creating good posts. There are many others out there who care about what you care about. As you build an audience, that will be clear. As you respond to that audience, you will learn more about their efforts, interests, and enthusiasms. It's about sharing. So if that acting role you just played excites you, tell people. As they respond to your enthusiasm, make sure to maintain the dialogue.

Being Found—a Word About Search on the Web

As I mentioned earlier, the concept of searchability is a big, complex topic. Being listed and listed well in search involves many aspects. From website design to content, back-end features, and much more, it takes an effort to be successful. Fortunately, the social media we discussed above have become very real drivers of the search functionality of search engines. Posting on social media sites can dramatically affect your visibility.

C. A. Tucker and his company, Artotems Co., deals with the new world of marketing every day. From design to consulting to social media management, they provide online marketing solutions that work. Artotems Co. cares about the work they do and whom they do it for. From actors studios in Florida and Louisiana to not-for-profit organizations working in Nepal, and many other business types, they help articulate and present their messages to the world and provide the support they need. Creativity is an engine of invention and delight in this world. They are happy to be part of it. If you want to contact Artotems Co., you will find them on the web at www.artotems.com.

Tara Brach on Buddhist Ancient Teachings

The Buddha's teaching came down to, "I teach about suffering and the end of suffering." He says that we suffer because we grasp on to a false understanding of what we want. Instead of being in touch with the truth of what matters, we clutch on to something smaller; we go for false substitutes and we can spin for decades, chasing after something that is not really going to meet our deep longing.

One of the zen masters, Sozuki-roshi, says that "the most important thing is remembering the most important thing." This is exquisite ,because any moment that we start really connecting with what our heart cares most about, we're home. D. H. Lawrence said that it's not what the "little self" wants, it is what the "deepest self" wants, and that takes some digging. You can ask people what they really want, but it takes a certain quality of presence to get in touch with what we truly desire, and you find that the more you get in touch with that, the more you commit to presence. The Buddha said that "the entire world unfolds on the tip of intention," and all of the Buddhist rituals, classes, and encounters start with aspiration.

It's the capacity to really be awake that reveals the gifts and the blessings in our lives. When you get in touch with your deepest desire, it doesn't compel you to look for something out there, it actually compels you to be right here. When we get in touch with what we really want, we realize it is always right here. The illusion is that what we long for is something out there, which is an endless wheel we are on. What we deeply desire is real contact and intimacy right here in this moment.

In the Buddhist teachings, we learn that we suffer because we are blocked from our deepest aspiration; we perceive ourselves as separate, and out of that separation comes clinging, grasping, and resistance. We feel that we're separate, so we cling on to another person versus opening and feeling the oneness that is already here. We resist intimacy because we feel like there is a threat, and we block the reality that the only real safety, the only real refuge, is in recognizing our oneness. As you start to see what really matters, you get underneath the illusion of separation.

On Living in the Present . . .

One of the great fruits of presence is spontaneity. In the Tibetan tradition they have what is called "the lion's roar," which is when you are at home with not knowing what's next. It is a courageous response to the moment that doesn't come out of the conceptual mind; it is instinctual. Your presence allows you to be in the flow, just the way a stream knows how to go around boulders. When you have entered the flow, your life springs out of this intuitive knowing and you respond appropriately to every moment. But what puts us apart from being in the flow is that we get caught in conceptual stories about ourselves and about the world that are static and fear-based.

The training to enter the flow is really a training to step out of your thoughts and come into the body. You approach this over and over again, until you begin to trust the intuition and the intelligence of the body itself. Part of the training is sensing the gap between thoughts and letting yourself rest in not knowing. This gets uncomfortable and edgy, but as you tolerate this uncomfortableness, you find that an aliveness springs forth, bringing you back into the flow, back into presence.

We are talking about an immersion of attention. You can get into the flow of writing or athletics or lovemaking or being in nature. There is a correlation of brain wave states that occurs when you are in the flow state, and this can actually be shown, where the brain waves shift from beta (the "fight/flight" mode) to alpha, which is correlated to well-being, happiness, peace, security, and creativity. I love the links to science and that science has shown this to be true.

The Path Towards Presence . . .

Internally, the training is to have the intention to notice when you leave presence. With meditation training you're saying, "My commitment is to keep coming back." You are coming back and you are training in being here; you are resting in the awareness that notices moment to moment what's happening, and you are letting go into the flow of experience. Externally, you are practicing to enter the flow with others, interpersonally, learning to spontaneously respond to situations. This is a coming into the body over and over and responding in a natural way.

Following is a primer on meditation for you. A lengthier primer can be found at www.tarabrach.com.

How to Meditate— a Guide to Formal Sitting Practice

What Is Meditation?

Meditation is commonly described as a training of mental attention that awakens us beyond the conditioned mind and habitual thinking, and reveals the nature of reality. In this guide, the process and the fruit of meditation practice is understood as Natural Presence. Presence is a mindful, clear recognition of what is happening here and now, and of the open space that includes all experience. There are many supportive strategies (called "skillful means") that create a conducive atmosphere for the deepening of presence. The art of practice is employing these strategies with curiosity, kindness, and a light touch. The wisdom of practice is remembering that Natural Presence is always and already here. It is the loving awareness that is our essence.

Approaching Meditation Practice

Attitude is everything. While there are many meditative strategies, what makes the difference in terms of spiritual awakening is your quality of earnestness, or sincerity. Rather than adding another "should" to your list, choose to practice because you care about connecting with your innate capacity for love, clarity, and inner peace. Let this sincerity be the atmosphere that nurtures whatever form your practice takes.

A primary aspect of attitude is unconditional friendliness toward the whole meditative process. When we are friendly toward another person, there is a quality of acceptance. Yet we often enter meditation with some idea of the kind of inner experience we should be having and judgment about not "doing it right." Truly, there is no "right" meditation, and striving to get it right reinforces the sense of an imperfect, striving self. Rather, give permission for the meditation experience to be whatever it is. Trust that if you are sincere in your intention toward being awake and openhearted, in time your practice will carry you home to a sense of wholeness and freedom. Friendliness also includes an interest in what arises, be it pleasant sensations or fear, peacefulness or confusion.

Creating a Container for Practice

It helps to have a regular time and space for cultivating a meditation practice. Morning is often preferred, because the mind may be calmer than it is later in the day. However, the best time is the time that you can realistically commit to on a regular basis. Some people choose to do two or more short sits, perhaps one at the beginning and one at the end of the day.

Deciding in advance the duration of your sit will help support your practice. For many, the chosen time is between fifteen and forty-five minutes. If you sit each day, you may experience noticeable benefits (e.g., less reactivity, more calm) and be able to increase your sitting time.

If possible, dedicate a space exclusively to your daily sitting. Choose a relatively protected and quiet space where you can leave your cushion (or chair) so that it is always there to return to. You may want to create an altar with a candle, inspiring photos, statues, flowers, stones, shells, and/or whatever arouses a sense of beauty, wonder, and the sacred. These are not necessary but are beneficial if they help create a mood and remind you of what you love.

It is helpful to recall at the start of each sitting what matters to you, what draws you to meditate. Take a few moments to connect in a sincere way with your heart's aspiration. You might sense this as a prayer that in some way dedicates your practice to your own spiritual freedom, and that of all beings.

Alertness is one of the two essential ingredients in every meditation. Sit on a chair, cushion, or kneeling bench as upright, tall, and balanced as possible. A sense of openness and receptivity is the second essential ingredient in every meditation, and it is supported by intentionally relaxing obvious and habitual areas of tension. Around an erect posture, let the rest of your skeleton and muscles hang freely. Let the hands rest comfortably on your knees or lap. Let the eyes close, or if you prefer, leave the eyes open, the gaze soft and receptive.

Please don't skip the step of relaxing/letting go! You might take several full, deep breaths, and with each exhale, consciously let go, relaxing the face, shoulders, hands, and stomach area. Or, you may want to begin with a body scan: start at the scalp and move your attention slowly downward, methodically relaxing and softening each part of the body. Consciously releasing body tension will help you open to whatever arises during your meditation.

The Basic Practice: Natural Presence

Presence has two interdependent qualities of recognizing, or noticing what is happening, and allowing whatever is experienced without any judgment, resistance, or grasping. Presence is our deepest nature, and the essence of meditation is to realize and inhabit this whole and lucid awareness.

We practice meditation by receiving all the domains of experience with a mindful, open attention. These domains include breath and sensations; feelings (pleasant, unpleasant, and neutral); sense perceptions, thoughts, and emotions; and awareness itself.

In the essential practice of meditation, there is no attempt to manipulate or control experience. Natural Presence simply recognizes what is arising (thoughts, feelings, sounds, emotions) and allows life to unfold, just as it is. As long as there is a sense of a self making an effort and doing a practice, there is identification with a separate and limited self. The open receptivity of Natural Presence dissolves this sense of a self "doing" the meditation.

Because our minds are often so busy and reactive, it is helpful to develop skillful means that quiet the mind and allow us to come home to the fullness of Natural Presence. These supports for practice help us to notice and relax thoughts and physical tension. They involve a wise effort that undoes our efforting.

You might consider yourself as a contemplative artist, with a palette of colors (supportive strategies) with which to work in creating the inner mood that is most conducive for the clarity and openness of presence. These colors can be applied with a light touch. Experiment and see what works best for you, and don't confuse these methods (such as following the breath) with the radical and liberating presence that frees and awakens our spirit. Regardless of what skillful means you employ, create some time during each sitting when you let go of all "doings" and simply rest in Natural Presence. Discover what happens when there is no controlling or efforting at all, when you simply let life be just as it is. Discover who you are, when there is no managing of the meditation.

You might take a few minutes at the beginning of the sitting (or anytime during the sitting or day) to intentionally awaken all the senses. Scan through the body with your attention, softening and becoming aware of sensations from the inside out. Listen to sounds, and also include the scent and the feel of the space around you in and outside of the room. While the eyes may be closed, still include the experience of light and dark, and imagine and sense the space around you. Explore listening to and feeling the entire moment-to-moment experience, with your senses totally open.

It is helpful to select a home base (or several anchors) that allow you to quiet and collect the mind, and to deepen embodied presence. Useful anchors are:

> The breath as it enters and leaves the nostrils.
>
> Other physical changes during breathing—e.g., the rise and fall of the chest.
>
> Other physical sensations as they arise—e.g., the sensations in the hands, or through the whole body.
>
> Sounds as they are experienced within or around you.
>
> Listening to and feeling one's entire experience (i.e., receiving sounds and sensations in awareness).

Mindfulness is the awareness that emerges through paying attention on purpose and nonjudgmentally to the unfolding of moment-to-moment experience. We train in mindfulness by establishing an embodied presence and learning to see clearly and feel fully the changing flow of sensations, feelings (pleasantness and unpleasantness), emotions, and sounds.

Imagine your awareness as a great wheel. At the hub of the wheel is mindful presence, and from this hub, an infinite number of spokes extend out to the rim. Your attention is conditioned to leave presence, move out along the spokes, and affix itself to one part of the rim after another. Plans for dinner segue into a disturbing conversation, a self-judgment, a song on the radio, a backache, the feeling of fear. Or your attention gets lost in obsessive thinking circling endlessly around stories and feelings about what is wrong. If you are not connected to the hub, if your attention is trapped out on the rim, you are cut off from your wholeness and living in trance.

Training in mindfulness allows us to return to the hub and live our moments with full awareness. Through the practice of "coming back," we notice when we have drifted and become lost in thought, and we recall our attention back to a sensory-based presence. This important capacity is developed through the following steps:

Set your intention to awaken from thoughts, mental commentary, memories, plans, evaluations, and stories, and rest in nonconceptual presence.

Gently bring attention to your primary anchor, letting it be in the foreground while still including in the background the whole domain of sensory experience. For instance you might be resting in the inflow and outflow of the breath as your home base, and also be mindful of the sounds in the room, a feeling of sleepiness, an itch, heat.

When you notice you have been lost in thought, pause and gently rearrive in your anchor, mindful of the changing moment-to-moment experience of your senses.

It can be helpful to remember that getting distracted is totally natural; just as the body secretes enzymes, the mind generates thoughts! No need to make thoughts the enemy; just realize that you have a capacity to awaken from the trance of thinking. When you recognize that you have been lost in thought, take your time as you open out of the thought and relax back into the actual experience of being Here. You might listen to sounds; re-relax your shoulders, hands, and belly; relax your heart. This will allow you to arrive again in mindful presence at the hub, senses wide open, letting your home base be in the foreground.

As the mind settles, you will have more moments of "being here,'" of resting in the hub and simply recognizing and allowing the changing flow of experience. Naturally the mind will still sometimes lose itself on the rim, and at these times, when you notice, you again gently return to the hub; "coming back," and "being here" are fluid facets of practice.

The more you inhabit the alert stillness at the center of the wheel and include in mindfulness whatever is happening, the more the hub of presence becomes edgeless, warm, and bright. In the moments when there is no controlling of experience, when there is effortless mindfulness, you enter the purity of presence. This is "Natural Presence." The hub, spokes, and rim are all floating in your luminous open awareness.

Here are a few helpful hints for sustaining your sitting practice:

Sit every day, even if it's for a short period. Intentionally dedicate this time of quieting—it is a gift to the soul!

A few times during each day, pause. Establish contact with your body and breath, feeling the aliveness that is Here.

Pause more and more—the space of a pause will allow you to come home to your heart and awareness.

Reflect regularly on your aspiration for spiritual awakening and freedom—your own and that of all beings.

Remember that, like yourself, everyone wants to be happy and nobody wants to suffer.

Practice regularly with a group or a friend.

Use inspiring resources such as books, CDs, or web-accessed dharma talks.

Study the Buddhist teachings (e.g., the four noble truths, the noble eightfold path).

Sign up for a retreat—one day, a weekend, or longer. The experience will deepen your practice and nourish spiritual awakening.

If you miss practice for a day, a week, or a month, simply begin again.

If you need guidance, ask for help from an experienced meditator or teacher.

Don't judge your practice; rather, accept what unfolds and trust your capacity to awaken and be free!

Live with a reverence for life, committed to non-harming—to seeing, honoring, and serving the sacred in all beings

Tara Brach is a leading western teacher of Buddhist meditation, emotional healing, and spiritual awakening. She has practiced and taught meditation for over thirty-five years, with an emphasis on vipassana (mindfulness or insight) meditation. Tara is the senior teacher and founder of the Insight Meditation Community of Washington. A clinical psychologist, Tara is the author of Radical Acceptance: Embracing Your Life with the Heart of a Buddha *and* True Refuge: Three Gateways of a Fearless Heart.

Tara is nationally known for her skill in weaving western psychological wisdom with a range of meditative practices. Her approach emphasizes compassion for oneself and others, mindful presence, and the direct realization and embodiment of natural awareness. You can learn more about Tara, and enjoy the many resources she offers, on her website: www.tarabrach.com.

About the Author

Larry Silverberg is one of the world's foremost authorities on the Sanford Meisner technique of acting through his internationally acclaimed four-volume series The Sanford Meisner Approach: An Actors Workbook and his book Loving to Audition. Larry also has two published books for teen actors, The 7 Simple Truths of Acting for the Teen Actor and Meisner for Teens: A Life of True Acting.

Larry is a graduate of the Neighborhood Playhouse School of Theatre, where he studied with legendary acting teacher Sanford Meisner. Since then, Larry has worked professionally as an actor and director across the United States and in Canada. Most recently, he received high praise from the New York Times for his performance as "Don" in Athol Fugard's People Are Living There at the Signature Theater in New York City, and he won the Seattle Critic's Association "Stellar Acting Award" for his portrayal of "Teach" in the Belltown Theatre Center production of American Buffalo.

Larry is founder and director of the True Acting Institute. Larry has been very busy touring Europe, Canada, South America, and the United States, teaching acting in his renowned professional actors training program, "The Meisner Master Class," which he brings to universities, colleges, and professional acting studios around the globe. Larry has also been teaching his "Teen Actor Master Class" at high schools all across the United States. Larry is available to lead symposiums and deliver keynote lectures on the Meisner technique and the craft of acting. In the summers, Larry leads his Meisner Certificate Training Program for actors, directors, and acting teachers.

Larry has also recently launched College Acting Programs. Com, his website devoted to helping high school actors find the best college acting programs. The website address is: www.collegeactingprograms.com.

Larry can be contacted through his website, www.trueactinginstitute.com.